VANCOUVER
Like a Local

BY THE PEOPLE WHO CALL IT HOME

VANCOUVER
Like a Local

BY THE PEOPLE WHO CALL IT HOME

Contents

NIGHTLIFE

OUTDOORS

meet the locals

LINDSAY ANDERSON
Lindsay is a writer and editor based in Vancouver. Her first book, FEAST: Recipes and Stories from a Canadian Road Trip, was published in 2017.

VIVIAN CHUNG
Lifestyle writer Vivian was born and raised in Vancouver. When she's not chasing a story, she's hiking the trails of B.C. or searching for her next donut.

ALEEM KASSAM
Design guru Aleem is a key fixture in Vancouver's interior design world. He's also a style icon and was named one of Canada's best dressed in 2017.

JACQUELINE SALOMÉ
Freelance writer Jacqueline fell in love with the city when studying here. Her interests collide at dawn, when she's either heading out for a hike or heading home from a rave.

MICHAEL WHITE
Former senior editor at Vancouver Magazine, Michael is now one half of the local food blog Jewkarta.

Vancouver
WELCOME TO THE CITY

Oh, Vancouver! Stunning snowcapped mountains, a temperate rainforest, and the Pacific Ocean kissing the shore: this laid-back city is perhaps best known for the natural beauty that surrounds it. And ever-active Vancouverites love nothing more than enjoying their backyard – on any day of the week, you'll catch them hiking, biking, or stand-up paddling, and that's before they even head to the office.

But there's more to this city than the great outdoors. Behind this wonderful natural playground is a cosmopolitan urban culture that's often overlooked. Vancouver is a glorious hodgepodge of cuisines, arts, industries, and cultures, from the First Nations whose lands the city occupies to a vibrant Asian diaspora making its own mark. Folks here are just as likely to visit a city art gallery as they are to jump in a kayak, to spend an evening on the dance floor as they are to run the full length of the Stanley Park Seawall.

It's not all sunshine and roses, though; life here isn't cheap, and it rains. A lot. But that doesn't dampen spirits. In fact, it's the perfect excuse to go out and support the local community. Expect to find locals indulging in hearty brunches in the city's cozy cafés, sipping hazy IPAs at craft breweries, and browsing charming bookstores where the warmest of welcomes awaits. The city's varied arts scene thrives, too, defying Vancouver's rep as "No Fun City."

Taking you through the cycle-friendly streets of the neighborhoods they live in, to the sushi joints, patio bars, and forested trails they adore, Vancouver's locals will let you in on the gems that make their city so livable (and lovable). So whether you're a Vancouverite looking to shake up your routine, or a visitor looking for inspiration, this book will show you the charms of the city. Strap in, and enjoy Vancouver like a local.

Liked by the locals

"Vancouver is like a small town wearing a big city's jacket. I love knowing my neighbors and local barista by name, and feeling like every area is only a short walk or bike ride away."

JACQUELINE SALOMÉ,
ARTS, CULTURE, AND TRAVEL WRITER

Spring cherry blossoms, summer beach parties, winter foodie festivals, and outdoor adventures year-round – there's always something afoot in Vancouver.

Vancouver
THROUGH THE YEAR

SPRING

PATIO SEASON
At the first glimpse of spring sunshine, locals have one thing in mind: patio season. Sitting out on a bar's terrace, enjoying a gulp of fresh air with a beer – life doesn't get better.

BLOSSOMS IN BLOOM
From late March to mid-April, Vancouver's 40,000 cherry trees erupt with dusty pink blossom. Don't miss the Cherry Blossom Festival, which hosts heaps of themed events.

A WHALE OF A TIME
After spending winter down south, thousands of whales migrate back to Vancouver's rich waters to feed and breed. Come May, it's prime salmon season for the orcas, making this the ideal time for a spot of whale watching.

SUMMER

OUTDOOR ADVENTURE
It's the moment that Vancouverites have been waiting for: adventure season. Whether it's hiking, surfing, bouldering, climbing, mountain biking, kayaking, or even base jumping, nothing can keep locals from their outdoor playground.

BEACH NIGHTS
Vancouverites spend the majority of their summer evenings on the beach picnicking and swimming with friends, catching the sunset, and biking home beneath the stars.

STREET PARTIES

Summer is festival season, and the city practically pulsates with life as major thoroughfares give way to indie music performances, pop-up disco parties, and foodie vendors. Don't miss the Khatsahlano Street Party in Kitsilano, Car Free Day in East Van, and the Mural Festival in Mount Pleasant.

FALL

CULTURE CRAWL

In November, artists, painters, jewelers, and makers in Vancouver's Eastside open their studios to the public for the annual Eastside Culture Crawl. Locals can't resist a peek behind the scenes.

A GOOD OL' HOCKEY GAME

Hockey is practically a religion here, and the love for the Vancouver Canucks runs deep, no matter how many times they lose. You'll know it's game day when Downtown becomes a sea of jersey-clad fans and hot dog stands.

THEATER SEASON

Sure, mainstream plays run year-round but, during fall, Vancouver's theater scene has a little more edge. The Arts Club Theatre Company and The Cultch start their runs, and the Vancouver Fringe and other festivals put on a calendar of comedy, dance, and cabaret performances.

WINTER

LET IT SNOW

It may not snow much in the city, but it sure does in the mountains. Come winter, outdoor enthusiasts shift their focus to ski and snowboarding season. Those who don't quite fancy hurling themselves down a mountain can still take advantage of gondola trips to enjoy the mountain views.

LATE NIGHTS

Forget what you heard about "No Fun City." When the rains come, Vancouverites trade their hiking boots for dancing shoes and hit the clubs.

DINE OUT FESTIVAL

In the winter months, over 300 of the city's best restaurants, wineries, and craft breweries come together to offer a fixed-price menu. It's a great opportunity to sample the city's best flavors at a more palatable price point.

There's an art to being a Vancouverite, from the do's and don'ts of eating out to negotiating the city's streets. Here's a breakdown of all you need to know.

Vancouver
KNOW-HOW

For a directory of health and safety resources, safe spaces, and accessibility information, turn to page 186. For everything else, read on.

EAT
Vancouver's foodie scene is as vibrant as it is varied — and one of its biggest claims to fame. Leisurely brunches are a weekend fixture, with the best places filling up early (get there before 10am to avoid lines). Brunch aside, locals eat pretty early, taking their lunches at 12pm, and sitting down for dinner any time from 6pm. Reservations are always a good idea, even on weekdays.

DRINK
Vancouver's cozy cafés and cool coffee shops are where locals come to catch up with friends, tap away on their laptops, or just take shelter from the rain. When it's time for something a little stronger, there are stylish cocktail joints, wine bars, and, of course, craft breweries. Taprooms and patios abound in areas like Mount Pleasant and East Van — most don't require a booking, but best avoid the 5pm rush.

SHOP
Vancouverites may be a practical bunch, but they have a strong sense of style. They love to support local makers and favor indie boutiques over chain stores. On weekends you'll find them browsing vintage, home decor, and outdoorsy stores anytime from 10am to 6pm when the stores close (5pm on Sundays). Tip: wherever you're parting with your paycheck, bring your own bag. You'll save yourself the charge of a paper one (which will just deteriorate in the rain).

ARTS & CULTURE

Most of Vancouver's galleries and museums charge $15–$30 for entry, but some offer special admission on certain days. Every Tuesday from 5pm to 9pm entry to the Vancouver Art Gallery is by donation only, so visitors can pay what they like. Entertainment venues will always require booking in advance, with special deals available through the year. Don't worry about dressing up, locals keep it pretty casual.

NIGHTLIFE

It may not be known as a party city, but Vancouverites love a night out. A small selection of club nights run through the week; Thursday, Friday, and Saturday nights are the busiest. There's also a strong LGBTQ2S+ scene in Vancouver (here in Canada, we use this acronym to include Two-Spirit, an Indigenous gender-fluid term). Places are generally open until 2am due to strict licensing laws, but if you're looking to keep the party going there are a handful of after-hours clubs that stay open until 7am. The catch? They don't serve booze.

OUTDOORS

Come rain or shine, locals flock to the city's many parks and beaches, or strike out farther afield to the nearby mountain trails to stretch their legs. And they're very protective of their natural spaces, so be sure to pick up your trash – pop it into a trash can or take it home with you from trails; there are hefty fines for leaving it behind.

Keep in mind

Here are some more tips and tidbits that will help you fit in like a local.

» **Tip well** Plan on tipping at least 15 per cent at restaurants and bars. Look at your check first; some places add gratuity.

» **Stay hydrated** Drinking water fountains are dotted around the city, parks, and beaches. You can also fill up at restaurants or cafés if you ask nicely.

» **No smoking** There's a strict ban on lighting up inside public buildings, as well as public parks, beaches, and patios.

» **Stay dry** It's no joke: Vancouver can sure get rainy. Keep an umbrella or rain jacket handy.

GETTING AROUND

Vancouver is pretty much surrounded by water, with the Pacific Ocean to the west, the Burrard Inlet to the north, and the Fraser River to the south. The city is divided into 22 distinct neighborhoods; North Vancouver, West Vancouver, and Richmond are separate municipalities.

The city follows a standard grid pattern, with most streets running north and south, and most avenues (which are usually numbered: 1st, 2nd, and so on) running east and west. Clear sightlines to the sea, rivers, and mountains that surround the city will always act as your compass.

Once you've got the city's pattern down, Vancouver is pretty easy to navigate, but, to help you along the way, we've provided what3words addresses for each sight in this book, so you can quickly pinpoint exactly where you're heading.

On foot

Vancouver is one of the most walkable cities in the world, and the main sights and neighborhoods are concentrated within a relatively small area. Tree-lined sidewalks take you to where you need to be, and the world's longest uninterrupted seaside greenway, known as the seawall, spans some 17 miles

(28 km), running all the way from the Vancouver Convention Centre to Spanish Banks Park on the Westside. It's a local favorite for running, biking, and taking an evening stroll.

Vancouverites are a pretty active bunch – you won't get far without a few keen runners whizzing by, so it's polite to leave plenty of space for them to pass. If you need to stop and check a what3words location, step to the side of the sidewalk to do so.

Sure, walking is less fun when it rains (which does tend to happen a lot), but don't let that put you off: just make like a local, pull on some boots and a rain jacket, and you're good to go.

On wheels

Depending on who you speak to, the locals either love or hate the city's cycle infrastructure. Cyclists are huge fans of the endless bikeways and dedicated cycle paths that run alongside most of the city's main roads. But many streets have been narrowed and, in some cases, roads have been closed to accommodate this, much to the chagrin of local drivers.

Mobi Bike, Vancouver's bike share scheme, has stations dotted throughout the city (you can pay per ride or it's $15 for unlimited rides in a 24-hour period), so you can pedal along scenic cycleways until your heart's content. Be sure to follow the rules of the road, such as obeying traffic signals, signaling when turning, and giving way to pedestrians – stick to the side of the path clearly marked for bikes rather than feet. Final rule: always, always wear a helmet. *www.mobibikes.ca*

By public transport

Vancouver's primary public transport system, Translink, makes getting around the city easy. Its extensive network of buses, skytrains, and sea bus services even connects Greater Vancouver to neighboring cities.

To pay, buy a Compass Card from any Translink station and pre-load the card with money. You can also pay by contactless or your phone. Remember to tap the same card when exiting. *www.compasscard.ca*

By car or taxi

Between walking, cycling, and public transport, there's little need to travel by car in town. For longer trips, rideshare apps like Uber and Lyft are available. Cabs are less common but, if that's more your style, Yellow Cab is a good option. If you do drive, be aware that parking spots can be scarce, and roads can get congested during rush hour.

Download these

We recommend you download these apps to help you get about the city.

WHAT3WORDS
Your geocoding friend
A what3words address is a simple way to communicate any precise location on earth, using just three words. ///sagging.protests.musical, for example, is the code for one of the totem poles in Stanley Park. Simply download the free what3words app, type a what3words address into the search bar, and you'll know exactly where to go.

CITYMAPPER
Your journey planner
Transportation apps for Vancouver can be a bit hit and miss, so locals prefer to use trusty old Citymapper. The route planner offers live info on the best routes to get from A to B, using buses, bikes, taxis, and more. There's reliable real-time info on departures and delays, too, which is always handy.

Vancouver is a tight hub of neighborhoods, each with their own distinct personality. Here, we take a look at some of our favorites.

Vancouver
NEIGHBORHOODS

Chinatown
Home to some of the city's hottest restaurants, traditional Asian bakeries, hip cocktail bars, and speakeasies, Chinatown is bold, brash, and unapologetic. It's also where much of the city's unhoused population resides. *{map 2}*

Coal Harbour
Towering glass condos offer an impressive backdrop to this glitzy marina, which is often abuzz with seaplanes and yachts ferrying diners to upscale restaurants. *{map 1}*

Downtown
Small but perfectly formed, Downtown is the city's commercial district. Here, locals browse shops on Robson Street, stop for a drink on Granville Street, and pop into Vancouver Art Gallery for some culture. *{map 1}*

East Van
Eclectic East Van is Vancouver's leftist liberal heart. Despite the slow but steady burn of gentrification, the area has maintained its bohemian attitude with edgy underground arts venues and indie restaurants peppered along The Drive. *{map 5}*

Fairview
Residential Fairview is crossed by the South Granville strip. Here, shoppers shock their wallets at high-end boutiques, which are popular with the mansion-dwellers of neighboring Shaughnessy. *{map 3}*

False Creek
All eyes are on False Creek, the last waterfront to see vast change. Though the patch is starting to undergo development, one cultural mainstay remains; Granville Island is an arts-abundant urban oasis with the city's biggest foodie market and best indie theaters. *{map 3}*

Gastown
One of Vancouver's oldest quarters (with cobbled streets to prove it), Gastown is anything but dated. Here, tourists and locals rub shoulders in boutiques and bars. *{map 2}*

Grandview-Woodland

This quirky quarter gets its cool cred from the young, modern beatniks drawn to the area's once-cheap rents. Think off-the-beaten-path breweries, indie theaters, and fabulous local restaurants. {map 5}

Kitsilano

A beachside paradise, Kitsilano is a year-round summer dream. You'll find everyone from college kids to stay-at-home parents all enjoying a refreshing swim in the neighborhood's stretch of ocean. {map 3}

Mount Pleasant

Once an industrial no-go zone, hipster-central Mount Pleasant is now a thriving community with an effortlessly cool vibe. There's street art aplenty here, and more small-batch craft beer breweries than you could ever visit in one lifetime. {map 4}

Olympic Village

This modern mini-city was developed to house athletes during the 2010 Vancouver Olympics. It's pretty quiet these days and mostly residential, but kayakers, dragon boaters, and watersports enthusiasts love it for its easy access to the water. {map 4}

Point Grey

Home to a popular stretch of sand between Jericho and Spanish Banks beaches, Point Grey offers the best vantage point to catch an epic Pacific sunset. Watching the sun sink with a cold one never gets old. {map 6}

Richmond

Just outside Vancouver lies Richmond – a diverse suburb that's home to the village of Steveston and some of the city's best Asian food, best sampled at the Richmond Night Market or on the Dumpling Trail. {map 6}

Strathcona

Historic Strathcona sits right by Downtown, but it offers a very different vibe; it's all about community in this residential patch. Neighbors wave at one another en route to their family-owned grocer before strolling to the park to meet friends for a picnic. {map 5}

UBC

The University of British Columbia (UBC) campus isn't just for students; it's the epicenter of many must-see attractions, from the Museum of Anthropology to the nudist haven of Wreck Beach. {map 6}

West End

Rainbow-colored Davie Village crosswalks make it easy to tell you're in Vancouver's historically queer quarter. The area's bars and bookstores are an extension of the home, and locals are vocal in their support. {map 3}

Yaletown

If you were under the impression that Vancouver is all Arc'teryx-wearing hikers and craft beer drinkers, Yaletown will set you straight. This warehouse district turned high-end and high-rise is the place for city sophisticates to see and be seen. {map 1}

*Strait of
Georgia*

<u>Vancouver</u>
ON THE MAP

*Whether you're looking for your new
favorite spot or want to check out
what each part of Vancouver has to
offer, our maps – along with our
handy map references throughout
the book – have you covered.*

0 kilometers	5
0 miles	5

0 meters 300
0 yards 300

WEST

**COAL
HARBOUR**

WEST

*Harbour
Green Park*

Digital Orca **Ⓐ**

GEORGIA

WEST HASTINGS STREET

WEST PENDER STREET

The Lobby
Lounge

Botanist **Ⓓ**

Ⓝ

ALBERNI

MELVILLE

STREET

The Marine Building

Ⓐ

WEST

CARDERO STREET

NICOLA STREET

WEST END

ROBSON STREET

STREET

Meat & Bread **Ⓔ**

BURRARD

HARO STREET

Kirin **Ⓔ**

HORNBY ST

WEST

BARCLAY STREET

NELSON STREET

STREET

The Wall
for Women
Ⓐ

DOWNTOWN

HOWE ST

STREET

Joe Fortes **Ⓔ**

Coast **Ⓔ Ⓔ** Thierry
Ⓓ

Bill Reid Gallery of
Northwest Coast Art **Ⓐ**

GRANVILLE ST

BROUGHTON STREET

COMOX STREET

JERVIS STREET

BUTE STREET

The Roof at
Black + Blue

The Pendulum
Gallery **Ⓐ Ⓓ** Reflections Terrace

Arc'teryx **Ⓢ**

Ⓐ Vancouver Art Gallery

**DAVIE
VILLAGE**

*Nelson
Park*

THURLOW STREET

Bacchus Lounge **Ⓓ**

ROBSON
SQUARE

Ⓓ 1931 Gallery
Bistro

Peacefu
Restauran

Ⓝ The Score on Davie

Ⓝ

Mary's on
Davie

Ⓝ 1181 Lounge
Ⓝ PumpJack Pub

DAVIE STREET

BURRARD STREET

HORNBY STREET

The Commodore **Ⓝ**
Ballroom

WEST GEORGIA

Cafe Medina **Ⓔ**

The Junction **Ⓝ**

ROBSON STREET

Numbers Cabaret **Ⓝ** **Ⓝ** The Fountainhead
Celebrities Nightclub **Ⓝ** Pub

HOWE STREET

STREET

The Basement &
Ⓝ The Living Room

SMITHE STREET

Maruhachi
Ra-men **Ⓔ**

Cinematheque **Ⓐ**

GRANVILLE STREET

PACIFIC STREET

Maxine's
Cafe & Bar **Ⓔ**

Fritz European Fry House **Ⓔ**
Twelve West **Ⓝ**

Scotiabank
Dance Centre

Ⓐ **Ⓐ** VIFF
Centre

HELMCKEN STREET

RICHARDS STREET

NELSON STREET

YALETOWN

SEYMOUR ST

Chancho **Ⓔ**
Tortilleria

HOMER ST

Ⓔ Blue Water Cafe

Mine & Yours **Ⓢ**

MAINLAND ST

The Spinning Chandelier **Ⓐ**

*Granville
Bridge*

Soho Bar & Billiards **Ⓔ** Tasty Indian
Ⓝ Bistro

PACIFIC BOULEVARD

Roundhouse Community **Ⓐ**
Arts & Recreation Centre

*David Lam
Park*

*Cooper
Park*

Heliport

WEST WATERFRONT ROAD

Portside Park

ALEXANDER ST

D Alibi Room

One of
a Few **S** **N** Herschel **S**
Ombre Show
Lounge **N** 2nd Floor
Gastown

WATER STREET

S Oak + Fort

John Fluevog
Shoes

Guilt & Co **N**

D Juice Bar

The Block **S**
Old Faithful Shop **S**
E.C. Rare Books **S**
Revolver **D**

GASTOWN

CAMBIE ST

Is That French **D**

E
Twisted Fork
Bistro
D The Diamond

S Kimprints

POWELL STREET

N Cantina
189 **D**
The **D**
Comedy Ring
Nemesis **D**

Collective **S**
Will

Hey Jude **S**

ABBOTT STREET

Greta Bar **N**
YVR

Kozak **E**

EAST CORDOVA STREET

COLUMBIA STREET

CARRALL STREET

Back and
Forth Bar **N**

D Pidgin

MAIN STREET

The Paper
Hound **S**

Victory
Square

Comedy **N**
After Dark

EAST HASTINGS STREET

N Calabash Bistro

CHINATOWN

WEST PENDER STREET

Skwachàys **A**
Lodge

BEATTY STREET

DUNSMUIR STREET

E Chambar

KEEFER
PLAZA

ABBOTT STREET

Chinese Canadian Museum

The Modern **S**
Bartender

EAST PENDER STREET

Fortune
Sound Club

E New Town
Bakery

Carriage
House

Bao Bei **D** **E** MILA

KEEFER PLACE

KEEFER STREET

Chickadee
Room

A
Dr. Sun Yat-Sen
Classical Chinese
Garden

Andy Livingstone
Park

QUEBEC STREET

DUNSMUIR STREET

EXPO VIADUCT

BOULEVARD

GEORGIA VIADUCT

PACIFIC BOULEVARD

Boxcar **D**
The American **N**

MILROSS AVE

MAIN STREET

0 meters   200
0 yards   200

MAP 2

🄴 EAT

Chambar *(p52)*
Kissa Tanto *(p53)*
Kozak *(p38)*
MILA *(p38)*
New Town Bakery *(p44)*
Phnom Penh *(p37)*
St. Lawrence *(p55)*
Twisted Fork Bistro *(p35)*

🄳 DRINK

Alibi Room *(p60)*
Bao Bei *(p83)*
Bar Gobo *(p68)*
Boxcar *(p66)*
Cantina 189 *(p80)*
Chickadee Room *(p65)*
The Diamond *(p83)*
Is That French *(p71)*
Juice Bar *(p68)*
Nemesis *(p73)*
Pidgin *(p81)*
Revolver *(p75)*

🅂 SHOP

The Block *(p96)*
Carriage House *(p101)*
Collective Will *(p102)*
E.C. Rare Books *(p89)*
Herschel *(p96)*

Hey Jude *(p102)*
Hunter & Hare *(p102)*
John Fluevog Shoes *(p97)*
Kimprints *(p93)*
Massy Books *(p91)*
The Modern Bartender *(p95)*
Oak + Fort *(p98)*
Old Faithful Shop *(p93)*
One of a Few *(p97)*
The Paper Hound *(p88)*

🄰 ARTS & CULTURE

Chinese Canadian Museum *(p113)*
Dr. Sun Yat-Sen Classical
   Chinese Garden *(p117)*
Firehall Arts Centre *(p127)*
Skwachàys Lodge *(p120)*

🄽 NIGHTLIFE

2nd Floor Gastown *(p139)*
The American *(p153)*
Back and Forth Bar *(p155)*
Calabash Bistro *(p139)*
Comedy After Dark *(p149)*
The Comedy Ring *(p150)*
Fortune Sound Club *(p145)*
Greta Bar YVR *(p152)*
Guilt & Co *(p136)*
Ombre Show Lounge *(p147)*
Paradise *(p145)*

0 meters 800
0 yards 800

Third Beach **O**

STANLEY PARK CAUSEWAY

Stanley Park **O**

Lost Lagoon

Second Beach

O Stanley Park Seawall

Coal Harbour

D Lift Bar & Grill

Tetsu Sushi Bar **E**

Momo Sushi **E**

The Sylvia Hotel Bar **D**

A-maze-ing Laughter **A**

N Chill Pill Comedy

WEST END

The Den **A** **N**

Roedde House Museum **A**

DENMAN ST

WEST GEORGIA STREET

English Bay Beach

NELSON STREET

ROBSON STREET

English Bay

DAVIE STREET

DAVIE VILLAGE

BURRARD STREET

HOWE STREET

SEYMOUR

217.5 Arc x 13 **A**

Sunset Beach and English Bay **O**

PACIFIC STREET

YALETOWN

Vancouver Maritime Museum **A**

Vanier Park

Museum of Vancouver **A**

Burrard Street Bridge

Kits Beach **O**

SUP at Kits Beach **O**

Granville Bridge

Whale watching **O** **A** Arts Club Theatre Company

Go Fish **E** **N** **A** Giants

The Improv Centre

False Creek

CORNWALL AVENUE

KITSILANO

Provide Home **S**

A Dalbergia Wood and Fine Objects

Charleson Park

MACDONALD ST

WEST 4TH AVENUE

Lululemon **S**

DUER **S**

Their There **D**

Arbutus Greenway **O** **E** **D** Grapes and Soda

Beaucoup

FAIRVIEW

WEST 6TH

OAK ST

ARBUTUS ST

WEST

BURRARD ST

BROADWAY

GRANVILLE ST

Glitch **N**

MAP 3

*Vancouver
Harbour*

3

EAT

Beaucoup *(p44)*
Go Fish *(p43)*
Momo Sushi *(p42)*
Tetsu Sushi Bar *(p42)*

Ⓓ DRINK

Grapes and Soda *(p71)*
Lift Bar & Grill *(p79)*
The Sylvia Hotel Bar *(p65)*
Their There *(p72)*
The Wicklow Pub *(p79)*

Ⓢ SHOP

DUER *(p106)*
Lululemon *(p105)*
Provide Home *(p95)*

Ⓐ ARTS &
CULTURE

217.5 Arc x 13 *(p131)*
A-maze-ing Laughter *(p129)*
Arts Club Theatre Company *(p124)*
Dalbergia Wood and Fine Objects
(p122)
Giants *(p130)*
Museum of Vancouver *(p114)*
Roedde House Museum *(p112)*
Vancouver Maritime Museum
(p119)

Ⓝ NIGHTLIFE

Chill Pill Comedy *(p151)*
The Den *(p155)*
Glitch *(p152)*
The Improv Centre *(150)*

Ⓞ OUTDOORS

Arbutus Greenway *(p164)*
Fishing Charter *(p171)*
Kits Beach *(p172)*
Stanley Park *(p160)*
Stanley Park Seawall *(p165)*
Sunset Beach and English Bay
(p175)
SUP at Kits Beach *(p168)*
Third Beach *(p174)*
Whale Watching *(p169)*

WEST HASTINGS ST
Waterfront
Station
DUNSMUIR ST

DOWNTOWN

BC
Place

Cambie Street
Bridge

Ⓞ Fishing Charter
Ⓓ The Wicklow Pub

CAMBIE ST

VENUE

WEST BROADWAY

False Creek

Cambie Street Bridge

Kayaking on False Creek **O**

TERMINAL AVENUE

OLYMPIC VILLAGE

Vancouver to Steveston **O**

B BETA5

S MEC

WEST 2ND AVENUE

Faculty **D** **E** Earnest Ice Cream

EAST 2ND AVENUE

MAIN STREET

A Emily Carr University of Art Design Galleries

N Jokes Please!

WEST 6TH AVENUE

D Bar Susu

The Matriarch
A

D Main Street Brewing Company

33 Acres **D**

The Fox Cabaret

N **N** **The Sunday Service**
Tightrope Theatre

Milano Espresso Bar **D**

E

WEST BROADWAY

Superbaba **S**

S Mintage Mall

D **S**
Modus Sports Junkies

F as in Frank **S**

EAST BROADWAY

Much & **S**
Little

MOUNT PLEASANT

WEST 12TH AVENUE

EAST 12TH AVENUE

KINGSWAY

MAIN STREET

E Burgoo

Harl
Ateli

WEST 16TH AVENUE

EAST 16TH AVENUE

S
Barter
Design

CAMBIE VILLAGE

Paragon **D**
Tea Room

E Rain or Shine

Sushi Hil **E**

PRINCE EDWARD STREET

FRASER STREET

S Walrus Design Inc

WEST 20TH AVENUE

Published on Main **E**

S The Main
Exchange

The Fish Counter **E**

Hero's Welcome **D** **S** The Regional Assembly of Text

S Lucky's Books & Comics

The Acorn **E**

WEST KING EDWARD AVENUE

EAST KING EDWARD AVENUE

SOUTH CAMBIE

MAIN STREET

RILEY PARK

E Trafiq

0 meters 500

0 yards 500

The Shameful **D**
Tiki Room

EAST 28TH AVENUE

CAMBIE STREET

MAP 4

4

🄴 EAT

The Acorn *(p32)*
BETA5 *(p46)*
Burgoo *(p36)*
Earnest Ice Cream *(p47)*
The Fish Counter *(p43)*
Published on Main *(p55)*
Rain or Shine *(p47)*
Superbaba *(p48)*
Sushi Hil *(p41)*
Trafiq *(p45)*

🄳 DRINK

33 Acres *(p61)*
Bar Susu *(p69)*
Faculty *(p62)*
Hero's Welcome *(p66)*
Main Street Brewing Company *(p60)*
Milano Espresso Bar *(p74)*
Modus *(p72)*
Paragon Tea Room *(p74)*
The Shameful Tiki Room *(p66)*

🅂 SHOP

Barter Design *(p94)*
F as in Frank *(p103)*
Harlow Atelier *(p92)*
Lucky's Books & Comics *(p91)*
The Main Exchange *(p100)*

MEC *(p106)*
Mintage Mall *(p103)*
Much & Little *(p95)*
The Regional Assembly of Text *(p92)*
Sports Junkies *(p105)*
Walrus Design Inc *(p94)*

🄰 ARTS & CULTURE

Emily Carr University of Art + Design Galleries *(p121)*
The Matriarch *(p130)*

🄽 NIGHTLIFE

The Fox Cabaret *(p137)*
Jokes Please! *(p148)*
The Sunday Service *(p149)*
Tightrope Theatre *(p148)*

🄾 OUTDOORS

Kayaking on False Creek *(p171)*
Vancouver to Steveston *(p167)*

STREET
WINDSOR
KINGSWAY
STREET
WINDSOR

D Settlement Building

DUNDAS STREET

D Straight & Marrow

Parallel 49 **D**

POWELL STREET

D Powell Brewing

COMMERCIAL DRIVE

Jackalope's
Neighbourhood Dive **D** **D** Dachi

EAST STREET

D Prototype

EAST HASTINGS STREET

The Heatley **N**

STRATHCONA

EAST VAN

HAWKS AVE

D Superflux

NANAIMO STREET

S ReLove Furniture

East Vancouver
Community Mural **A**

D Caffe La Tana

MAIN STREET

E Hunnybee
Bruncheonette

O
Adanac
Bike Route

PRIOR STREET

VENABLES STREET

Downlow **E**
Chicken Shack

Strathcona
Park

Pacific
Central
Station

Parker **A**
Street Studios

CLARK DRIVE

D Moja

E Via Tevere

Moon Based **N**
Comedy

**GRANDVIEW-
WOODLAND**

To Live For **E**
Bakery

TERMINAL AVENUE

Bar Corso **D**

EAST 1ST AVENUE

COMMERCIAL DRIVE

VICTORIA DRIVE

NANAIMO STREET

NORTH

**MOUNT
PLEASANT**

GRANDVIEW HIGHWAY

EAST BROADWAY

The Rio **A**

EAST 12TH AVENUE

PRINCE EDWARD STREET

FRASER STREET

EAST 15TH AVENUE

KINGSWAY

KNIGHT STREET

Clark Park

Trout Lake
Park

VICTORIA DRIVE

NANAIMO STREET

EAST

E House of Dosas

EAST KING EDWARD AVENUE

0 meters   800
0 yards   800

**KENSINGTON-
CEDAR COTTAGE**

KINGSWAY

VICTORIA DRIVE

MAP 5

5

HASTINGS ST

HASTINGS-SUNRISE

🄴 EAT

Downlow Chicken Shack *(p48)*
House of Dosas *(p50)*
Hunnybee Bruncheonette *(p35)*
To Live for Bakery *(p46)*
Via Tevere *(p36)*

🄳 DRINK

Bar Corso *(p69)*
Caffe La Tana *(p70)*
Dachi *(p70)*
Jackalope's Neighbourhood Dive *(p64)*
Moja *(p73)*
Parallel 49 *(p62)*
Powell Brewing *(p62)*
Prototype *(p75)*
Settlement Building *(p64)*
Straight & Marrow *(p83)*
Superflux *(p61)*

🅂 SHOP

ReLove Furniture *(p100)*

🄰 ARTS & CULTURE

East Vancouver Community Mural *(p130)*
Parker Street Studios *(p120)*
The Rio *(p126)*

🄽 NIGHTLIFE

The Heatley *(p136)*
Moon Based Comedy *(p151)*

🄾 OUTDOORS

Adanac Bike Route *(p167)*

RENFREW STREET

EAST BROADWAY

22ND AVENUE

Renfrew Park

Kite- and Windsurfing in Squamish
26 miles (42 km)

HORSESHOE BAY

Whyte Lake

Cypress Provincial Park

Lynn Headwaters Regional Park

Capilano River Regional Park

Lynn Canyon

Fisherman's Trail

EAGLE HARBOUR

WEST BAY

Sandy Cove Beach

WEST VANCOUVER

CAPILANO

LYNN VALLEY

Lighthouse Park

Ambleside

NORTH VANCOUVER

Inter River Park

SEYMOUR HEIGHTS

The Polygon Gallery

Spirit Trail

Burrard Inlet

Taiga Works

English Bay

7A

Museum of Anthropology

Jericho and Spanish Banks

The Galley Patio and Grill

POINT GREY

See maps 1–5 for Central Vancouver

7

The UBC Arts & Culture District

Beaty Biodiversity Museum

Wreck Beach

UBC

1

Pacific Spirit Regional Park

The Patty Shop

DUNBAR

Banh Mi Saigon

Vessi

Hill's of Kerrisdale

Shameless Buns

KERRISDALE

KILLARNEY

Musqueam Cultural Centre

Original Tandoori Kitchen

SUNSET

MARPOLE

Gallery

Mitchell Island

Vancouver Airport

EAST CAMBIE

Continental Seafood Restaurant

91

RICHMOND

SOUTHARM

Fraser River

TILBURY

STEVESTON

Gulf of Georgia Cannery

Village Books & Coffee House

0 kilometers 3

0 miles 3

MAP 6

EAT

Known for its booming and beloved culinary scene (and fittingly foodie locals), Vancouver is a city where anything goes — from high-end seafood spots to cozy ramen bars.

Brunch Spots

If ever there was a meal that epitomizes Vancouver's laid-back, take-it-easy vibe, it's brunch. Too late for brekkie, too early for lunch, late weekend mornings are perfect for feasting at the city's food joints.

THE ACORN

Map 4; 3995 Main Street, Mount Pleasant; ///stumble.belt.slogans; www.theacornrestaurant.ca

Have your phone at the ready – the dishes at The Acorn are pic-worthy pieces of art. Happily, the all-vegetarian dishes here not only look beautiful but taste great, too. There's a focus on locally foraged and farmed ingredients, often showcasing the more unusual side of British Columbia's natural bounty. Case in point: the German butter potatoes with tree salt, fir mustard, kelp ketchup, and relish. Yum.

CAFE MEDINA

Map 1; 780 Richards Street, Downtown; ///unable.prongs.subjects; www.medinacafe.com

Everyone and their next-door neighbor knows Medina. The bad news? Getting a table requires some serious strategic planning. And the good news? The effort is totally worth it. Every plate of food lives up to Medina's legendary reputation, with North African, Mediterranean, and Middle Eastern flavors offering a little bit of zing to favorites including sausages and halloumi.

» Don't leave without ordering the Belgian waffles for dessert. No matter how full you are, they're an absolute must.

CONTINENTAL SEAFOOD RESTAURANT

Map 6; 11700 Cambie Road, Richmond; ///arrow.master.infuses; www.continentalrestaurant.ca

Locals may be partial to a good old eggs Benedict of a weekend, but for many it's the promise of *har gow* (shrimp dumplings) that gets them out of bed. At Richmond's Continental Seafood Restaurant, the dumplings are served the old-fashioned way; staff wheel carts laden with fresh dim sum between tables. Simply flag one down and take your pick of these Cantonese treasures.

Just outside of Squamish is the rural Sunwolf Resort. Here, beside the resort's river, is Fergie's *(https://fergiescafe.ca)*, the most Canadian of brunch joints. Most customers eat outside (weather permitting, of course), tucking into eggs benny and French toast in a mountain setting that's almost comically idyllic. While you're waiting for a table, take a wander down to the river and plunge your hands into the glacial water – it's even more of a wake-up than that first cup of Fergie's coffee.

Solo, Pair, Crowd

Solo brunching? Need some morning sustenance with the gang? Whatever the crowd, Vancouver has you covered.

FLYING SOLO
Burrow down at the bar
Like your brunch with a side of feel-good vibes? Make for The Burrow, a community-minded veggie and vegan café. Settle in and watch as plates of tofu scramble, cornbread bennies, burritos, and huevos rancheros slide through the pass.

IN A PAIR
Table for two
Yolks has two locations in Vancouver, both ideal spots for a small, quiet table. Order a couple of freshly squeezed orange juice cocktails and the truffle lemon potatoes to share.

FOR A CROWD
Hang with the gang
Reserve a table for you and your friends at Homer St. Cafe and Bar. With mimosas by the pitcher, this is the place to start the weekend with a bang.

MAXINE'S CAFE & BAR

**Map 1; 1325 Burrard Street, West End; ///outraged.jetted.stocky;
www.maxinescafebar.com**

It may be relatively new on the scene, but Maxine's already has that
classic, bistro-that's-been-here-forever vibe. Don your best jeans and
sneakers and join West End regulars for a (loosely) French-inspired
brunch, including steak tartine, linguine frittata, and plenty of frites.
» Don't leave without ordering Canada's brunch staple, a punchy
Caesar cocktail (made with vodka, tomato juice, and clam broth).

TWISTED FORK BISTRO

**Map 2; 213 Carrall Street, Gastown; ///spades.trendy.pipes;
https://forkandfriends.ca**

The morning after a big night out, bleary-eyed locals make a beeline
for the Twisted Fork. Not only are its big plates of baked eggs, golden
rosti, and banana-stuffed brioche French toast the perfect hangover
comfort food, but there's an entire section of the drinks menu entitled
"Hair of the Dog." Breakfast here is just what the doctor ordered.

HUNNYBEE BRUNCHEONETTE

**Map 5; 789 Gore Avenue, Strathcona; ///homing.enter.using;
www.hunnybeebrunch.com**

No matter the day, this airy space is filled with a steady stream of
beanie-clad locals refueling after a bike ride or yoga class. Follow
their lead and order the stewed shakshuka or one of the café's
renowned breakfast sandwiches topped with herb aioli.

Comfort Food

A pessimist would say that Vancouver has miserably rainy winters, period. An optimist, however, would say that without the cold, damp weather, the city would never have gotten so good at making comfort food.

BURGOO

Map 4; 3096 Main Street, Mount Pleasant; ///direct.protest.clusters; https://burgoo.ca

From day one, Burgoo set out to offer the good people of Vancouver the most comforting of comfort foods from around the world. And it's safe to say it's succeeded. Locals return time and again to sample soothing and familiar dishes like mac and cheese, beef bourguignon, *elotes* (Mexican street corn), and famously good biscuits in a space that's as cozy as a hand-sewn quilt.

VIA TEVERE

Map 5; 1190 Victoria Drive, Grandview-Woodland; ///bouncing.hook.twisting; https://viateverepizzeria.com

Emitting an invitingly warm glow, Via Tevere tempts local East Van pizza lovers like moths to a flame. The restaurant's servers have been here forever (always a good sign) and their skilled *pizzaioli*

If you're buying a pie for a picnic, bring your own pizza cutter/ knife/scissors – they're always unsliced.

produce exceptional wood-fired pizza. It's just about everything a good neighborhood pizza restaurant should be and more.

PHNOM PENH

Map 2; 244 E Georgia Street, Chinatown; ///dandelions.assume.banter; https://phnompenhrestaurant.ca

Has there been a day this place *hasn't* had a lineup since it opened in 1985? A Chinatown institution in a neighborhood that's seen a great deal of change, Phnom Penh offers consistently excellent Vietnamese-Cambodian cuisine. Proudly family-run, with a friendly crowd of regulars, this feels like a true home away from home.

» Don't leave without trying the uber-famous butter beef and the equally renowned crunchy/salty chicken wings.

ORIGINAL TANDOORI KITCHEN

Map 6; 7215 Main Street, Punjabi Market; ///fended.cheat.mailbox; https://originaltandoorikitchen.com

Huddled under their umbrellas, hungry locals make their way to Original Tandoori Kitchen for a winter warmer with spice and smoke. This welcoming joint is a stalwart of Punjabi Market – the epicenter of Vancouver's Indo-Canadian community – and its traditional clay tandoor oven is as inviting as any hearth. Settle in for a feast of smoky naan breads and homestyle Indian classics like *shahee paneer*, a dish of fresh cheese simmered in a silky blend of tomatoes and cream.

KOZAK

**Map 2; 1 W Cordova Street, Gastown; ///fail.papers.testing;
www.kozakeatery.ca**

As soon as Kozak's doors swing open, you're hit with the mouth-watering aromas of simmering pierogi, steaming pots of borscht, freshly baked bread, and cottage cheese pancakes frying on the grill. It's a combination that's especially satisfying on a cold day, though you'll find Kozak's loyal customers – including Ukrainian expats craving a taste of home – visiting all months of the year.
» Don't leave without taking a few (hefty) slices of the Brooklyn-style chocolate babka to go.

MILA

**Map 2; 185 Keefer Street, Chinatown; ///turned.promise.whispers;
www.milaplantbased.com**

In need of a long overdue catch-up with an old friend? Bring them to MILA. They're sure to be delighted by this trendy but unpretentious space, serving diverse favorites like oshi sushi,

Try it!
DUMPLING TRAIL

If dumplings are your thing, Tourism Richmond *(www.visitrichmondbc.com)* has multiple "Dumpling Trail" itineraries throughout the city of Richmond, easily accessible from Vancouver by Skytrain.

flavor-packed bao, "fish" tacos, dan dan noodles, and peanut butter cup pie. In fact, the latter is so good, next time your pal will be the one inviting you to MILA's sister vegan pizza joint just around the corner.

MARUHACHI RA-MEN

Map 1; 270 Robson Street, Downtown; ///textiles.puppets.baseline; https://maruhachi.ca

According to local ramen fans (of which there are many in this city), you can taste the difference between each of Maruhachi's six chain locations. Is that true? Who knows. But this is for sure: whether you're a seasoned expert or new to Maruhachi altogether, you're sure to fall for the signature Tori-Paitan (a style of creamy chicken broth that the restaurant pioneered). Our pick of the branches is the Central Library location – it has the heartiest broth, we swear.

FRITZ EUROPEAN FRY HOUSE

Map 1; 718 Davie Street, Downtown; ///stunts.diet.compound; (604) 684-0811

When it comes to comfort food, you can't do better than Canada's most famous dish, poutine – a glorious concoction of French fries topped with cheese curds and smothered in gravy. After a long day in the city, Fritz is exactly the right place to get some. And, hey, if "some" doesn't seem like quite enough, you can always opt for the portion size simply called "bucket." Pro tip: see those holes in your seat's armrests? They've been handily designed for holding your giant cone of fries.

Seafood Spots

Think Vancouverites never get riled up? Ask a group of locals to name the city's best sushi joint. People here are passionate about seafood (we're by the Pacific, after all), and chefs go out of their way to source the best.

JOE FORTES

Map 1; 777 Thurlow Street, Downtown; ///stared.response.succeed; www.joefortes.ca

A bit of advice: some locals may tell you that only tourists go to Joe Fortes. Ignore them. There's a reason this two-level palace of brass and checkerboard tile has been packing the crowds in since 1985. Loud, snazzy, and more than a little bit kitsch, it's a place to channel your inner Mad Man with a long lunch of B.C. oysters on the half shell and a bottle of crisp white wine.

KIRIN

Map 1; 1172 Alberni Street, Downtown; ///hippy.pigs.retina; www.kirinrestaurants.com

By day, Kirin might not seem like much of a seafood place (the extensive lunch menu offers treats of a meatier variety). Come evening, though, it's a different story. The dinner menu is a shellfish lover's dream, packed with specialties like lobster (retrieved live from the in-house tank), abalones, shrimp, and scallops prepared in dozens of ways, all with a north Chinese twist.

COAST

Map 1; 1054 Alberni Street, Downtown; ///sleeping.trendy.slimmer; www.glowbalgroup.com/coast

"Go big or go home" seems to be the guiding principle at Coast. The restaurant itself is huge, seating over 250 people. The giant circular oyster-and-cocktail bar pours out a seemingly endless stream of classic aperitifs. And with around 50 options at any given time, the food menu offers an entire ocean's worth of variety. Overwhelmed by the options? The ultra-decadent, multi-tiered seafood tower will check every box and then some.

» Don't leave without ordering the lobster bisque. In an ideal world, all soups would taste like this.

SUSHI HIL

Map 4; 3330 Main Street, Mount Pleasant; ///stops.however.port; www.sushihil.com

Given that there are literally hundreds of sushi joints in Vancouver, it takes a lot for one to stand out. Yet from the second it opened in 2022, Sushi Hil was a big deal. Why? Well, there's chef Hil Nguy, who prizes freshness and flawless presentation above all else, for one thing. And for another, it's a lovely, cozy space. It feels both casual and ceremonial – like you know you're in for something special (and you are).

MOMO SUSHI

Map 3; 833 Bidwell Street, West End; ///gliding.hoofs.risk; www.momosushibidwell.com

On a budget and in a hurry? Momo is the place to go. Despite offering over 100 items – including rolls, nigiri, and sashimi, plus rice bowls and bento boxes – everything is tasty, affordable, and ready in minutes. There aren't many seats, but that's not a problem; get takeout and enjoy in nearby Stanley Park or on the seawall.

BLUE WATER CAFE

Map 1; 1095 Hamilton Street, Yaletown; ///batches.sheet.photo; www.bluewatercafe.net

Sitting down to dinner at Blue Water, with its antique-style lamps and crisp white tablecloths, feels like arriving at the captain's table. It's a splurge (in case the visiting Hollywood celebs didn't give it away), but it's worth forgoing this month's rent money. You'll be amazed by the freshness and quality of the dishes, from sablefish in an umami miso-sake glaze to raw shellfish served on ice.

TETSU SUSHI BAR

Map 3; 775 Denman Street, West End; ///unroll.animals.rope; www.tetsusushibar.com

What Tetsu lacks in size, it more than makes up for in reputation. This four-table (plus four-seat bar) shrine to raw fish was named one of Canada's 100 best restaurants in 2022. And as soon as one piece of chef Satoshi Makise's sashimi melts on your tongue, you'll

Takeout is an option at Tetsu, but try to sit in for an "omakase" experience, with dishes chosen by the chef.

understand why. Like Makise himself, all the fish here heralds from Japan – the menu changes daily depending on what is caught and shipped across the seas.

GO FISH

Map 3; 1505 W 1st Avenue, Granville Island; ///emperor.offline.juggler

Yes, you're going to have to stand in line. And yes, it will be worth it. This little tin shack, right next to the water near Granville Island, has been so popular for so long that it doesn't bother with a website or social media. Every week, without fail, hundreds wait patiently for incredible fried to-order fish and chips, grilled salmon tacos, and assorted seafood sandwiches. On a sunny day, it's a quintessential Vancouver experience – just watch out for hungry seagulls.

» Don't leave without checking out nearby Granville Island Public Market, a gastronomic wonderland of local produce.

THE FISH COUNTER

Map 4; 3825 Main Street, Mount Pleasant; ///less.insist.observe; www.thefishcounter.com

All hail chef Robert Clark, a local hero who basically kick-started the West Coast sustainable seafood movement and cofounded this top-notch fish market. Vancouverites show their gratitude by flocking here on weekends for fish and chips, crab-and-shrimp baguettes, and dairy-free clam chowder. Find a quiet corner under the wooden beams inside, or join the locals on a shared bench out front.

Sweet Treats

There's no denying this city has a sweet tooth; even with all the hiking, biking, and marathon-ing taking place, a good pastry is (fortunately) just as easy to find as a nutritious green juice.

BEAUCOUP

Map 3; 2150 Fir Street, South Granville; ///fend.liners.biked; www.beaucoupbakery.com

What's better than a classic French pâtisserie? A classic French pâtisserie with a Chinese twist, that's what. At Beaucoup, siblings Betty and Jacky Hung draw on their culinary roots to make a cornucopia of addictive treats, like buttery pastries and decadent cookie sandwiches. Delicacies like mango crêpe croissants – a play on the traditional dim sum specialty – are worth the trip alone.

NEW TOWN BAKERY

Map 2; 148 E Pender Street, Chinatown; ///workforce.pastime.system; www.newtownbakery.ca

For more than four decades, New Town Bakery has been filling East Pender Street with the sweet, custard-y aroma of its Chinese and Filipino treats. Follow your nose (and the stream of takeout

Saint Germain is another popular Chinese bakery with multiple locations across Vancouver.

customers) and pick up some cocktail buns for a mid-afternoon snack. They may look like fancy hot dog buns, but inside they ooze with a sweet coconut paste.

THIERRY

Map 1; 1059 Alberni Street, Downtown; ///briefers.risks.round; https://thierrychocolates.com

Stepping into this chic pâtisserie is like entering an art gallery. Glass cases gleam with neat rows of meticulously made pastries and desserts, each more beautiful than the last. Take the petite, crimson-colored Raspberry Sevigne, for instance; this mirror-glazed dome of sponge is soaked with lemon juice and topped with raspberry mousse and fresh raspberries. It's almost too good-looking to eat (but, no, really, you should eat it).

» Don't leave without ordering a cup of Thierry's indulgently thick hot chocolate – it's a no-brainer on a cold, winter day.

TRAFIQ

Map 4; 4216 Main Street, Riley Park-Little Mountain; ///caved.steamed.writers; https://trafiq.ca

In between browsing Main Street's vintage stores, shoppers pop into this welcoming little spot for a restorative treat. The go-to snack with their coffee? It's a tough call between the Chunky Monkey bread pudding (don't judge appearances) and the mousse-filled Homage to Earl Grey cake. Maybe just order both to be safe?

BETA5

Map 4; 409 Industrial Avenue, Strathcona; ///kneeled.blizzard.flexed; https://shop.beta5chocolates.com

Unless your car gets towed, there's no way you'll accidentally stumble upon BETA5. Found next to the city's impound lot, just off Main Street, this boundary-pushing company is famous for its sustainable chocolates and wildly beautiful cream puffs in flavors like mango milk tea and lychee rose.

TO LIVE FOR BAKERY

Map 5; 1508 Nanaimo Street, Grandview-Woodland; ///potato.flat.jigsaw; https://tolivefor.ca

This sun-filled vegan bakery began with a humble loaf of banana bread. Local influencer Erin Ireland baked the treat as a gift for friends and family when her funds were tight. It was met with such

Shh!

Coffee shops? Vancouver has plenty of those. But coffee shops where the donuts are better than a cappuccino? Much more rare – and 49th Parallel Cafe *(https://49th coffee.com)* knows it. With a small bakery tucked away out back, it turns out trays of apple bacon fritters, maple bars, French cruller pastries, and a host of other treats. Donuts can be eaten in-house or taken away by the baker's dozen, because you'll want to try every flavor going.

glowing praise that Erin began selling her baked goods, developing an array of cookies, pastries, and cupcakes. Now a word-of-mouth sensation, Erin's banana bread is truly the gift that keeps on giving.

EARNEST ICE CREAM

Map 4; 1829 Quebec Street, Mount Pleasant;
///beamed.relaxing.crowned; https://earnesticecream.com

For a famously rainy city, Vancouver has a *lot* of good ice cream. And it's all thanks to pioneering places like Earnest. Since it began serving scoops from a cargo bike back in 2012, Earnest has become a city institution. It's tricky to pin down what we love most, from the growing list of plant-based flavors to the partnerships with community organizations. This is a lesson in good local ice cream done right.

» **Don't leave without** attempting to get your hands on a pint of Earnest's spruce tip ice cream – yes, it's made with literal trees.

RAIN OR SHINE

Map 4; 3382 Cambie Street, Cambie Village;
///dweller.pets.farmer; http://rainorshineicecream.com

Earnest, or Rain or Shine? The debate is fierce among the city's ice-cream connoisseurs. One thing everyone can agree on, though, is that Rain or Shine does some great seasonal specialties – like fresh B.C. corn, plum sherbet, vegan pumpkin pie, and genmaicha rice puff. Plus, Taco Tuesdays are awesome: two scoops of ice cream served in a crunchy waffle taco shell, topped with whipped cream and various crunchy additions. Yes, please.

Cheap Eats

Vancouver may be an expensive place to live, but high price tags don't always extend to food. From self-serve counters to casual sit-downs, there are plenty of places offering quality eats on a budget.

SUPERBABA

Map 4; 2419 Main Street, Mount Pleasant; ///visions.scared.share; www.vancouver.eatsuperbaba.com

There's a lot of hype around this quick-serve Middle Eastern joint, and for good reason. Crispy eggplant is fried to order, fluffy pita bread is served fresh from the oven, and smoky chargrilled chicken wraps are drizzled with herby sauces. Need even more convincing? Try the sumac mayo and shug, a regional serrano pepper-based hot sauce with garlic and cilantro. It's nothing short of smokin'.

DOWNLOW CHICKEN SHACK

Map 5; 905 Commercial Drive, East Van; ///oblige.dollar.shears; www.dlchickenshack.ca

Why is Vancouver so obsessed with fried chicken? Some might say it's down to this place. Southern-style eats are cooked to perfection here, with a recipe that produces beautifully crispy, juicy, and undeniably

 If fried chicken is your thing but gluten isn't, check out Juke Fried Chicken, in Chinatown, instead. addictive chicken every single time. Between the deep-fried wings and boneless thighs, the saucy chicken breast sandos are the crowd faves.

BANH MI SAIGON

Map 6; 5397 Victoria Drive, Kensington-Cedar Cottage;
///drew.thrones.conclude; www.banhmisaigon.ca

If you're guaranteed one thing at this family-run (and cash-only) spot, it's bang for your buck. Banh Mi Saigon never skimps on portion sizes, tucking generous medleys of cold cuts and pickled radish into golden baguettes. Groups of colleagues flock here, making the most of the buy-10-get-one-free offer. A warning, though: with its consistently long line, this isn't exactly "fast" food.

PEACEFUL RESTAURANT

Map 1; 602 Seymour Street, Downtown;
///runs.engages.restriction; www.peacefulrestaurant.com

After a tough day on the trails, a reviving bowl of dan dan noodles at Peaceful is the perfect tonic. Here, owner and head chef Charlie Huang whips up comforting northern Chinese dishes, with each plate of steaming dumplings or bowl of fried rice a celebration of bold Chinese flavors. And the best part: the bountiful portion sizes mean a feast won't break the bank.

» **Don't leave without** scarfing down a hefty basket of tasty *xiao long bao* (soup dumplings) alongside your noodles.

HOUSE OF DOSAS

Map 5; 1391 Kingsway, Kensington-Cedar Cottage;
///warm.replace.teams; (604) 875-1283

For many locals, a Monday isn't complete without a trip to this
South Indian favorite. Dubbing it "Dosa Day," at the start of every
week, House of Dosas slashes the price of its namesake dish (a thin
dal pancake filled with savory stews) to just $5.99. It's a tasty deal,
and one you'll find hard to resist once you've gorged on one (or two)
of those sensational lamb vindaloo or lentil specials.

CHANCHO TORTILLERIA

Map 1; 560 Davie Street, Downtown;
///puts.value.colonies; www.chancho.ca

This may look like your classic no-frills joint (picture red-and-white
checkered tables and plastic garden chairs), but Chancho Tortilleria
has an ace up its sleeve. The folk here know that the tortilla is the key
to a perfect taco, so they make theirs in-house using corn sourced
from various Indigenous communities in Oaxaca. Just take a bite of
that pork belly taco and you'll taste the love that's gone into it.

SHAMELESS BUNS

Map 6; 5772 Fraser Street, Sunset; ///trails.trample.fields;
www.shamelessbuns.com

Filipino cuisine didn't have much of a stronghold in Vancouver
until husband-and-wife duo Matt and Corvette rocked up with this
cheerful restaurant. Now, locals flock here for unusual delights such

as *lumpia* (Filipino-style spring rolls), spam fries, and chicken adobo. The pair also serve the masses via their colorful food truck – check the Shameless Buns socials to see where it's heading next.

THE PATTY SHOP
Map 6; 4019 Macdonald Street, Arbutus Ridge;
///debating.vital.coiling; (604) 738-2144

You might be surprised to hear that one of Vancouver's foodie hot spots is hidden in the family-friendly neighborhood of Arbutus Ridge. Here, the tiny Patty Shop has been a gathering place for the students and staff of nearby schools since the McHardy family opened it in 1979. Little has changed: Jamaican patties are still the order of the day, Daryl McHardy still serves the staple flavors of his Caribbean childhood, and the locals still stop by for a daily snack.

» Don't leave without picking up a few extra packs of patties for later – our favorite has to be the curry beef.

MEAT & BREAD
Map 1; 1033 W Pender Street, Coal Harbour;
///hips.target.diggers; www.meatandbread.com

Slices of roast meat are served between fresh ciabatta bread at this decidedly hipster, but refreshingly affordable, sandwich shop. Signature offerings include the crispy porchetta, meatball, and buffalo chicken sandwiches. Meat & Bread sees the biggest lines each December, when the famous Turducken sandwich (a glorious turkey, duck, and chicken trifecta) hits the menu.

Special Occasion

In a city that favors comfort over glamour, even fine dining is a laid-back affair. Prefer sneakers to heels? You're in good company. Celebrating Vancouver-style simply means great food with great people.

CHAMBAR

Map 2; 568 Beatty Street, Crosstown; ///pity.pirates.dairy; www.chambar.com

Nowhere typifies the city's relaxed dining scene quite like Crosstown's Chambar. Head chef Nico Shuerman might have cooked for such illustrious figures as Mick Jagger and Bill Clinton, but his modern bistro is all about casual, homespun simplicity. The moules frites and braised lamb shank with honey, figs, and cinnamon are still our first pick for a perfect date night.

TASTY INDIAN BISTRO

Map 1; 1261 Hamilton Street, Yaletown; ///crawling.nipped.kneeled; www.tastybistro.ca

Hidden away at the quiet southern end of Hamilton Street, this darkly luxurious space is a favorite among families and friends with something to celebrate – especially around the time of Diwali.

Groups chat animatedly as they pass around paneer tacos and plates of classic curry, before finishing it all off with the divine cardamom layer cake. When it comes to good-time vibes and friendly faces, we can guarantee this place is number one.

KISSA TANTO

Map 2; 263 E Pender Street, Chinatown; ///sands.vibrate.younger; www.kissatanto.com

Chef Joël Watanabe started Kissa Tanto with an enviably simple idea. He fused two of Vancouver's best-loved cuisines: Italian and Japanese. The result is one of the city's coolest restaurants and toughest reservations. Happily, despite its reputation, the swanky joint still manages to feel laid-back, with the late-night vibe of a 1960s Tokyo jazz bar. And the food is just as classy — even a simple burrata salad gets a surprising twist, leaving little doubt that Italian and Japanese food is the perfect pairing.

>> **Don't leave without** toasting the occasion with something from the extensive selection of Japanese whiskeys and sakes.

Try it!
COOK UP A STORM

Planning to make a special dinner at home? Whether you're hopeless in the kitchen or a seasoned pro, you'll learn some valuable new tricks in the classes at The Dirty Apron Cooking School (*www.dirtyapron.com*).

Liked by the locals

"To me, a quintessential 'special occasion' restaurant in Vancouver is Miku; it's got an amazing view of the harbor, and few things speak to Vancouverites' collective sense of taste than sushi and sashimi. Everything we've ever eaten there has been outstanding."

M'BETH JACOBSEN, VANCOUVER RESIDENT

MIKU

Map 1; 70–200 Granville Street, Coal Harbour; ///winks.another.juggle; www.mikurestaurant.com

Glamorous sushi on the waterfront, anyone? If you still need convincing, let's just point out that dinner here is as much about the location as it is about the theater of watching blowtorch-wielding chefs prepare aburi oshi sushi. This house specialty is pressed and then flame-seared for a smoky, explosively delicious mouthful.

ST. LAWRENCE

Map 2; 269 Powell Street, Japantown; ///bashed.leave.nibbles; www.stlawrencerestaurant.com

There's a reason why everyone's obsessed with St. Lawrence. The menu is a love letter to French-Canadian cuisine, with each classic inspired by chef Jean-Christophe Poirier's upbringing in Quebec. And with an effortlessly understated atmosphere, what's not to love? **» Don't leave without** making sure you try the signature fried pork rinds flavored with maple syrup and Montreal steak spice.

PUBLISHED ON MAIN

Map 4; 3593 Main Street, Mount Pleasant; ///donation.wrong.cobble; www.publishedonmain.com

Not only was Published on Main one of the first places in the city to receive a Michelin star, it's also been voted Canada's best restaurant. Here, familiar ingredients like asparagus or local halibut are turned into picture-perfect dishes. This is just what paydays were made for.

A foodie afternoon
in East Van

For authentic global flavors, indie East Van is where it's at. Since the 19th century, this patch of the city has seen waves of immigration, with Chinese, Southeast Asian, and European settlers choosing to call it home. Today, folks come here to sample delicious sushi, Vietnamese Phở, Portuguese custard tarts, and Canadian staples worth writing home about. This tour takes in some of the area's best-loved foodie hotspots, from family-owned grocers to trendy-without-trying diners you won't want to miss – trust us.

1. Hunnybee Bruncheonette
789 Gore Avenue; www.hunnybeebrunch.com
///homing.enter.using

2. Union Market
810 Union Street;
www.unionmarket.ca
///patrol.playful.ship

3. Fujiya
912 Clark Drive; www.fujiya.ca
///clots.chipper.thirsty

4. Superflux
505 Clark Drive;
www.superfluxbeer.com
///gasping.cheeks.bleach

5. Lunch Lady
1046 Commercial Drive;
www.thelunchlady.com
///brand.denote.value

The Gourmet Warehouse
///gown.leaves.detained

POWELL STREET
STRATHCONA

Grab brunch at HUNNYBEE BRUNCHEONETTE
Enjoy a slow start to the afternoon with a brunch of stewed shakshuka, ricotta pancakes, and a cheeky glass of ice cold Aperol Spritz slush.

UNION STREET

PRIOR STREET

TERMINAL AVENUE

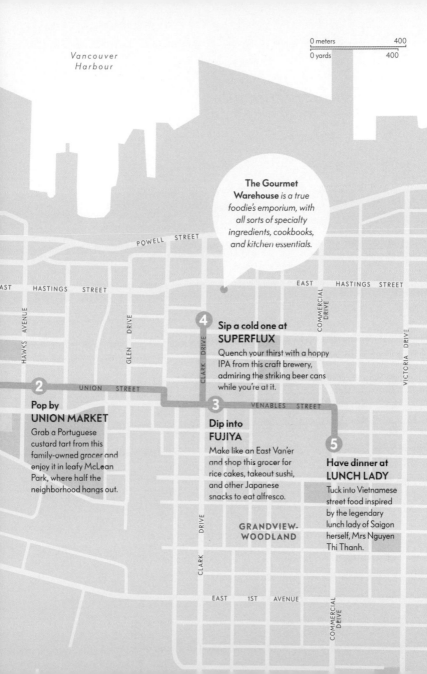

Vancouver
Harbour

0 meters 400
0 yards 400

POWELL STREET

The Gourmet Warehouse *is a true foodie's emporium, with all sorts of specialty ingredients, cookbooks, and kitchen essentials.*

EAST HASTINGS STREET

EAST HASTINGS STREET

HAWKS AVENUE

GLEN DRIVE

CLARK DRIVE

COMMERCIAL DRIVE

VICTORIA DRIVE

4 Sip a cold one at
SUPERFLUX
Quench your thirst with a hoppy IPA from this craft brewery, admiring the striking beer cans while you're at it.

2 UNION STREET

Pop by
UNION MARKET
Grab a Portuguese custard tart from this family-owned grocer and enjoy it in leafy McLean Park, where half the neighborhood hangs out.

3 VENABLES STREET

Dip into
FUJIYA
Make like an East Van'er and shop this grocer for rice cakes, takeout sushi, and other Japanese snacks to eat alfresco.

5

Have dinner at
LUNCH LADY
Tuck into Vietnamese street food inspired by the legendary lunch lady of Saigon herself, Mrs Nguyen Thi Thanh.

CLARK DRIVE

GRANDVIEW-WOODLAND

CLARK

EAST 1ST AVENUE

COMMERCIAL DRIVE

DRINK

The endless months of rain here aren't all bad – they give locals the perfect excuse to hunker down with a drink in the city's cozy bars and hipster cafés.

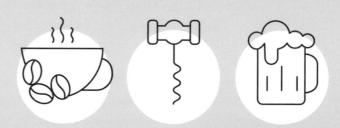

Breweries

Ever since the 2012 craft beer explosion birthed over 40 breweries and counting, beer drinking has become a way of life in Vancouver – especially in the epicenters of East Van (aka Yeast Van) and Mount Pleasant.

MAIN STREET BREWING COMPANY

Map 4; 261 E 7th Avenue, Mount Pleasant; ///parade.recently.youthful; www.mainstreetbeer.ca

Fun fact: back in the city's pre-Prohibition heyday, Mount Pleasant was known as Brewery Creek. Today, that legacy lives on via Main Street Brewing, which serves crisp classics and old-school cask ales from a beautiful heritage brewery built in 1913.

ALIBI ROOM

Map 2; 157 Alexander Street, Downtown Eastside; ///laptop.rides.reapply; http://alibi.ca

Okay, it's not a brewery, but this is hands-down Vancouver's best beer bar, with 50 rotating taps. Always bustling with beer fans looking to try something new, this is a spot where you won't annoy your server by describing your nebulous taste preferences and asking for their recommendation. Dark beer, but make it fruity? Something from

The Alibi team also runs Brassneck Brewery in Mount Pleasant and The Magnet in Gastown.

Field House for you. Sour, but dry-hopped? Try Nectarous by Four Winds. You'll find exactly what you didn't know you were looking for.

SUPERFLUX

Map 5; 505 Clark Drive, East Van; ///gasping.cheeks.bleach; www.superfluxbeer.com

Superflux burst onto the scene in 2015 and almost instantly became Vancouver's hop headquarters – an impressive feat in a city that's absolutely fanatical about IPAs. Serving beer that tastes as good as the cans containing it look, this cool East Van watering hole is the spot to shock your lager-loving taste buds with high intensity hops.

33 ACRES

Map 4; 15 W 8th Avenue, Mount Pleasant; ///requested.swam.bench; https://33acresbrewing.com

One of the original Mount Pleasant breweries, minimalist 33 Acres is a neighborhood fave. And for good reason. The brewery's flavorful mainstay beers – 33 Acres of Ocean, 33 Acres of Life, 33 Acres of Sunshine, and 33 Acres of Darkness – keep regulars content, while the unusual concocotions from the Brewing Experiment next door (hello, Mezcal Gose) lure those with more adventurous palettes.

» Don't leave without starting your day with the mouth-watering brunch. The menu changes weekly, but you can expect inventive takes on classics like waffles and smashed avocado on toast.

PARALLEL 49

Map 5; 1950 Triumph Street, East Van; ///napkins.husbands.shears;
http://parallel49brewing.com

No, you're not in an airport – it's just a flight board-style screen
displaying dozens of beers, offering you a one-way ticket to inebriation.
Don't overthink it. Just pick the brew that appeals the most and soak
up the vibe of this lively East Van institution, indoor food truck and all.

POWELL BREWERY

Map 5; 1357 Powell Street, Downtown Eastside; ///enable.likely.harmless;
www.powellbeer.com

Don't judge this modest tasting room by its looks; Powell's charming
line of great beers and respected barrel-aging program wows more
than interior decor ever could. The friendly barhops will gladly
oblige with a flight of their favorites.

» Don't leave without trying the award-winning Old Jalopy Pale
Ale, the beer that shot Powell Brewing to success.

FACULTY

Map 4; 1830 Ontario Street, Mount Pleasant; ///huddled.vows.famed;
www.facultybrewing.com

At Faculty, there's no such thing as a secret family recipe. Instead, the
beermaker publicly shares its brewing process, so beer lovers can
learn about what they're drinking and then make it themselves. And if
home brewing isn't your thing, there's always home delivery – Faculty is
a partner in The BeerVan, which brings drinks right to your door.

Liked by the locals

"Over the past decade, Vancouver has exploded with breweries. You can easily find your favorite beer style without even having to stray too far outside your neighborhood – people love drinking local."

JESSICA SHARPE, PARTNER IN SLOW HAND BREWING
AND THE BEERVAN

Local Bars

Vancouver doesn't just do comfort food – it does comfort bars, too. The city overflows with characterful watering holes, which act as second homes for their devoted regulars.

JACKALOPE'S NEIGHBOURHOOD DIVE

Map 5; 2257 E Hastings Street, East Van;
///entry.delivers.obstruction; https://jackalopesdive.com

When "dive" is in the actual name, you know you're going to get some grunge. And yep, Jackalope's is a mishmash of thrifted light fittings, framed music posters, and a steady soundtrack of rock and heavy metal. The drinks menu continues the theme: expect jello shots, pitchers of lager, and fishbowl cocktails to share.

SETTLEMENT BUILDING

Map 5; 55 Dunlevy Avenue, Railtown; ///blaze.alien.octopus;
www.settlementbrewing.com

It's easy to walk right past this unassuming white building in Railtown, but behind its wooden doors you'll find something special. Here, you get two bars for the price of one – beer-focused Settlement Brewing and grape-heavy Vancouver Urban Winery (plus popular restaurant Belgard Kitchen thrown in for good measure). And they both make their own tipples on site, too. Join happy-hour regulars sipping the afternoon away, in a beautiful open-plan space that's cozy as heck.

CHICKADEE ROOM

Map 2; 182 Keefer Street, Chinatown; ///deposits.gamer.wiping; https://thechickadeeroom.com

Tucked inside popular Juke Fried Chicken, this teeny-tiny space may just be the smallest bar in the city. Find cheerful revelers squished around the wooden tables, sipping on complex cocktails (featuring unusual ingredients like black lime and black sesame syrup, spiced horchata, and toasted coconut) and snacking on the obligatory fried chicken, of course.

THE SYLVIA HOTEL BAR

Map 3; 1154 Gilford Street, West End; ///lend.highways.sisters; https://sylviahotel.com

The historic Sylvia Hotel has been charming Vancouverites ever since it opened the city's first cocktail bar in 1954. It's a visual treat: thick ivy carpets the hotel's walls, turning it a vibrant green in summer, before exploding into crimson reds and fiery oranges come fall. The cherry on top? The bar's sparkling views of English Bay. No wonder it's a favorite with local romantics.

» Don't leave without watching carefully for ghosts. Errol Flynn is rumored to haunt the halls, despite having died elsewhere in Vancouver.

BOXCAR

Map 2; 923 Main Street, Strathcona; ///sleeper.quicker.revived;
www.boxcarvancouver.com

About the width of a boxcar (hence the name), this ultra laid-back speakeasy is a bar of two halves. Inside, it's dark and divey – think distressed wood walls and a long line of stools squeezed next to the bar. Out back, it's a different story, with a huge, bright-blue patio and pastel-pink tables. Both spaces hum with the chatter of relaxed groups, catching up over craft beer and creative cocktails.

THE SHAMEFUL TIKI ROOM

Map 4; 4362 Main Street, Riley Park; ///thorax.parting.drive;
https://shamefultikiroom.com

When they're missing the sunshine in the depths of the gray winter gloom, the city's vitamin D-deprived locals make their way to the Shameful Tiki Room. Draped in palm fronds, wooden masks, and puffer fish lamps, it's like stepping foot on a tropical island. A live surf band and ukulele players only add to the good vibes – as do the rum-based cocktails featuring pineapple, coconut, and lime.

HERO'S WELCOME

Map 4; 3917 Main Street, South Main; ///youngest.distract.retained;
https://heros-welcome.com

They say that a bar can be the heart of a community, and Hero's Welcome is living proof of that. For 71 years, this spacious pub was the home of the Army, Navy, & Air Force Veterans Club, until it closed in 2019. When the owners of Hero's Welcome took over the space in 2021, they were determined to honor this legacy. Not only do photographs, uniforms, and flags on the walls pay tribute to the bar's history, but the affordably priced food and drinks continue its blue-collar spirit. If the crowd of old-timers and neighborhood newbies is anything to go by, they've done South Main proud.

BACCHUS LOUNGE

Map 1; 845 Hornby Street, Downtown, ///bike.goat.smiling; www.wedgewoodhotel.com

With its roaring fire, brass-trimmed wingback chairs, velvet sofas, and candlelit atmosphere, Bacchus admittedly isn't the best choice at the height of summer. But as soon as the cold weather hits, it's the most popular place in the city. Order a Charter House cocktail (made with Chartreuse and hot chocolate) and snuggle up with your significant other to the soothing sounds of live piano music.

>> Don't leave without trying your absolute darndest to claim the fireside seats. (Order some truffle fries to celebrate once you do.)

Try it!
BARTEND UP A STORM

Want to re-create your favorite bar experience at home? Take a class at Brandywine Bartending School (www. brandywine.ca) and learn the secrets of wine tasting and cocktail mixing.

Wine Bars

With the vineyards of British Columbia's Okanagan Valley only a stone's throw away, Vancouver's wine bars are well stocked with flavorful pours, newly released from the vineyard.

BAR GOBO

Map 2; 237 Union Street, Strathcona; ///situated.battling.song; www.bargobo.com

Bar Gobo is tiny. Like, really tiny. So much so that the "kitchen" is a small workstation at the end of the bar. But it all just adds to the irresistible energy and "Come on in!" friendliness of this cozy spot. There's a definite wine nerd vibe about the place (and we mean that as a compliment), with staff eager to tell you about whatever's new and exciting. They know their stuff so listen to them.

JUICE BAR

Map 2; 54 Alexander Street, Gastown; ///glee.latest.miracle; www.juicebaryvr.com

By day, it's a well-loved café called The Birds & the Beets. At 4pm, however, cups of coffee are swapped for glasses of natural wine (made with organic or biodynamic grapes) and the space transforms

Ask at the Juice Bar for anything by Sunday in August. The B.C. winery always knocks it out of the park.

into this combination bar and bottle shop. The whole place buzzes with loud, happy conversation, as the post-work crowd kick back with a glass of the city's finest.

BAR SUSU

Map 4; 209 E 6th Avenue, Mount Pleasant; ///rock.deputy.cheater; www.thisisbarsusu.com

In late 2021, the owners of Published on Main *(p55)* decided they wanted to open a casual wine bar. And why not? Giving a dumpy beer hangout a bit of spit and polish, they've created one of the hottest places in town. Chic but relaxed, it's an intimate space that's just as good for trying to impress a date as it is for a hangout with your best friends.

» Don't leave without trying the French-influenced small plates. The signature Duck Liver Parfait is a gourmet delight.

BAR CORSO

Map 5; 1566 Commercial Drive, East Van; ///eminent.requested.panel; www.barcorso.ca

It may be in the heart of Vancouver's Little Italy, but don't expect any old-school trattoria vibes here. No, Bar Corso is reinterpreting the neighborhood's Italian heritage for the next generation. And what does that look like? A clean, sleek room packed with 20- and 30-somethings, enjoying the 100-per cent Italian wine list and shareable snacks like salumi and crostini.

CAFFE LA TANA

Map 5; 635 Commercial Drive, East Van; ///pausing.shapes.outbid; www.caffelatana.com

There are few places in Vancouver where it feels appropriate to drop in, drink a glass of excellent wine, and be on your happy way. At this little spot, though, you can do just that. Caffe La Tana is less your typical wine bar and more of a casual European café, complete with marble counter, checkerboard floor, and shelves of Italian groceries for sale. The irony is that it's so inviting, you'll find yourself wanting to linger with a whole bottle.

DACHI

Map 5; 2297 E Hastings Street, Hastings-Sunrise; ///online.roaming.homes; www.dachivancouver.com

Dachi means "pal" in Japanese, and the welcome you'll receive here is as warm and hearty as that of an old friend. The staff are happy to chat about anything and everything, while an unpretentious crowd of neighborhood folks make it feel like

Try it!
LOCAL TASTES

Want to know what the locals are drinking? Head to one of the five branches of Liberty Wine Merchants (*www.libertywinemerchants. com*). The selection at each store is curated specially for the local neighborhood.

you're a guest at a lively dinner party. Oh, and did we mention that all of the wines are natural, organic, and/or biodynamic? They're all from small, family-owned wineries, too, which only adds to the community vibe.

» **Don't leave without** buying a bottle to take home – Dachi's bottle shop is one of the most interesting in Vancouver.

IS THAT FRENCH

Map 2; 45 Blood Alley Square, Gastown; ///selects.forced.unwanted; (604) 681 1111

Yep, you read the address right: Is That French is located in Blood Alley (an actual alley that can look about as inviting as it sounds). Don't be put off by the location, though – this trendy, industrial-style space serves an expert selection of natural wines. On any given evening, you'll find couples sipping on glasses of pinot gris, while pals share delicious small plates of oysters and local cheeses.

GRAPES AND SODA

Map 3; 1541 W 6th Avenue, South Granville; ///chained.retrial.noodle; www.grapesandsoda.ca

Wondering where Vancouver got its natural wine obsession from? Look no further than this place. On a quiet side street where it doesn't look like anything interesting should be happening, this loud, energetic sliver of a room started a city-wide revolution. By-the-glass selections change often, but there's always something delicious from B.C.'s Okanagan Valley.

Coffee Shops and Cafés

Like Seattle and Portland to the south, Vancouver loves its coffee. No matter where you are in the city, you can't chuck a reusable coffee cup without hitting a good café.

MODUS

Map 4; 112 W Broadway, Mount Pleasant; ///bespoke.urge.rock; www.moduscoffee.com

Nothing flashy to see here. Just a quiet, cute space staffed by nice people who take their coffee seriously. (We're talking good beans from ethical suppliers and a scientific balance of strength and temperature.) The pour-overs are perfect fuel for shopping on nearby Main Street.

THEIR THERE

Map 3; 2042 W 4th Avenue, Kitsilano; ///blurts.became.alert; www.theirthere.ca

The attention to detail at this coffee and brunch spot is truly something to behold. Why? Well, for one thing, the lattes and Americanos are dispensed with utmost care by baristas who seem to genuinely love what they do. For another, the donuts are so uncommonly pretty you'll want one of each (pray they have the raspberry cheesecake mochi flavor). Plus, the plant-filled room is straight out of a trendy design magazine. No wonder it's perpetually slammed.

» Don't leave without getting the Smash Burger (available Fridays to Sundays), the best burger you'll ever have in a coffee shop.

NEMESIS

Map 2; 302 W Hastings Street, Gastown;
///hounded.exacted.monument; www.nemesis.coffee

When a coffee break calls, Vancouver Film School students and local shopworkers make a beeline for this tastefully minimalist, nearby café. Not only does it serve serious coffee (its website painstakingly details where it sources its beans), but it also sells some of the best pastries in the city. Pair the epic tiramisu croissant with an expertly poured latte and enjoy the room's crackling urban energy.

MOJA

Map 5; 1102 Commercial Drive, East Van; ///soccer.armful.truth;
www.mojacoffee.com

Moja started almost 20 years ago, when two friends hatched a plan in a North Vancouver basement. Fast-forward to now and their roasting business is so successful that they've also opened this bustling, sun-filled café. It's basically a shrine to coffee, with a huge roaster and long shelves of beans and accessories. Caffeine addicts of all stripes make a daily pilgrimage here, from exhausted parents to busy students.

PARAGON TEA ROOM

Map 4; 3361 Cambie Street, Cambie Village; ///shell.rattler.stereos;
www.paragontearoom.com

Coffee not your caffeine fix of choice? You want Paragon. This
modern take on an old-fashioned tea salon attracts folks from across
the city for its extensive selection of hot and iced teas, including
matcha, bubble teas, mistos, and more. The baked goods – like
bubble waffles and brioche donuts – are equally knockout.

MILANO ESPRESSO BAR

Map 4; 156 W 8th Avenue, Cambie-Broadway;
///putter.checked.outbid; www.milanocoffee.ca

Long before North American coffee culture was really a thing,
Milano's aim was to bring the excellence of hand-roasted Italian
coffee to Vancouver. The locals loved it, and there are now eight

Shh!

Tucked away on a quiet,
tree-lined residential street,
in the converted storefront of
what used to be a family home,
is the utterly charming Le
Marché St. George *(www.
marchestgeorge.com)*. At any
given time, the sidewalk out
front is filled with local residents
fortifying themselves with
great coffee, flaky croissants,
quiche, and more. Bonus:
it's also a general store,
where you can stock up on
condiments, cheeses, and
drinks for a sunny-day picnic.

locations in B.C. and Alberta – but the West 8th branch is the original (and the best). It's wonderfully spacious, with views of the park across the street and a neighborly mix of families, students, and local workers all enjoying their morning cup.

PROTOTYPE

Map 5; 883 E Hastings Street, Strathcona; ///reward.camp.examples; www.prototypecoffee.ca

Arguably Vancouver's most unique-looking café (all that dark wood and sculptural greenery makes it feel like you're arriving for a spa day), this spotless, ultra-modern space is a veritable coffee destination. It's both a "tasting room" and a self-contained production facility, with more than 14 different coffees available at any given time. You're bound to love at least one, especially in combination with a house-made waffle donut (just as good as it sounds).

REVOLVER

Map 2; 325 Cambie Street, Gastown; ///acrobat.sound.informs; www.revolvercoffee.ca

Don't be surprised to find a line out the door at this buzzy Gastown spot. Why? It's simple, really: the coffee is exceptional. It's so good, in fact, that this is where employees of other cafés go on their day off. Join them in the line and watch the baristas prepare reviving pour-overs with all the solemnity of a beautiful religious ritual.

» Don't leave without selecting a bag of beans to take home from Revolver's scrupulously curated inventory.

Rooftops and Patios

Long ago, Vancouver made a deal with the weather: in exchange for the disheartening amount of rain that falls during winter, the city will have gorgeously lush patios available to imbibers all summer long.

1931 GALLERY BISTRO
Map 1; 750 Hornby Street, Downtown; ///cold.guarded.unfair; www.1931gallerybistro.com

Sitting atop the Vancouver Art Gallery *(p116)*, this lovely little oasis is as pretty as the pictures inside. (Think lots of leafy palms and elegant cypress trees.) It's a favorite afternoon drink spot with art fans, shoppers, and lunching friends, who come to revive with art-inspired tipples like Banksy in the Bramble and Wei Wei Winter Sangria. Our tip? Ask for a corner seat so you can people-watch over bustling Robson Square.

THE GALLEY PATIO AND GRILL
Map 6; 1300 Discovery Street, West Point Grey; ///quiz.lashed.directly; https://thegalley.ca

This casual self-serve patio, at the Jericho Sailing Center above Locarno Beach, was tailor-made for balmy mornings and deliciously drawn-out afternoons. Sip craft beer and gorge on beachside

The Galley doesn't take reservations, but there's usually a good chance of a free patio spot mid-afternoon.

classics like burgers, fish and chips, and chowder while watching the sailboats go by. With the sound of the waves lapping gently against the shore, it's sheer bliss.

REFLECTIONS TERRACE

Map 1; 801 W Georgia Street, Downtown; ///museum.octopus.duke; www.rosewoodhotels.com

Dressed-to-impress influencers love the high-profile rooftop patio at Hotel Georgia. And who can blame them? In the summer months, it's a lush space with appropriately themed cocktails like the Secret Garden Fizz and the Rosewood Garden Tree; come winter, it transforms into a wonderland of tinsel and twinkling lights. Which is prettier? You'll just have to try both to find out.

D/6 BAR & LOUNGE

Map 1; 39 Smithe Street, Yaletown; ///veal.respond.units; www.parqvancouver.com

D/6 is the epitome of bougie rooftop cool. Up on the sixth floor of the Parq Vancouver hotel, this indoor-outdoor cocktail bar is a see-and-be-seen kind of place, with swanky decor and a fashionable post-work crowd sipping drinks like the Billionaire Martini (made with truffle vermouth, no less). It's the location that steals the show, though – the patio feels like it's magically suspended between the skyscrapers.

» Don't leave without checking out the Hidden Lounge – a secret bar hidden behind a bookcase inside.

Solo, Pair, Crowd

Whatever your company, Vancouver's patios will wow you with the city's stunning natural beauty.

FLYING SOLO
Leisurely stroll
After taking a contemplative wander through the immaculately manicured botanical gardens at Van Dusen, The Garden Cafe is the perfect place to kick back with a coffee.

IN A PAIR
Secret hideout
The Arbor on Main Street has one of the neighborhood's best-kept secrets — an impossibly green, garden-like patio. Sit with a friend among the plants and order some wine and creative vegan plates.

FOR A CROWD
Stay a while
Gather the gang for a lazy afternoon at the Pac Rim Patio (in front of the Fairmont Pacific Rim). Enjoy harborside views and a festival-style mix of cocktails, live music, and an upscale food truck.

LIFT BAR & GRILL

**Map 3; 333 Menchion Mews, Coal Harbour; ///journals.forget.arrived;
www.liftbarandgrill.com**

Perched at the edge of the shimmering waters of the Burrard Inlet,
with views of Stanley Park's thick forests and the coastal mountains
beyond, this is the West Coast patio of dreams. Add in cozy firepits
and spectacular sunsets, and it's got everything you need for a
romantic date or anniversary celebration.

THE ROOF AT BLACK + BLUE

**Map 1; 1032 Alberni Street, Downtown; ///stacks.assist.supple;
https://blackandbluesteakhouse.ca**

Unless you really dig the sides of buildings, the rooftop at Black +
Blue doesn't have the best views. But who cares when you're sat
beneath a beautiful flower-festooned pergola? Complete the stylish
mood with a classic cocktail like a negroni or Sazerac.

» Don't leave without taking advantage of happy hour, which runs
daily from 2:30 to 5:30pm.

THE WICKLOW PUB

**Map 3; 610 Stamps Landing, False Creek; ///certainty.sleeper.faster;
www.thewicklow.com**

Come summer, cyclists, joggers, and dog walkers pounding the seawall
can't help but pause at the patio outside The Wicklow Pub. Right
on the waterfront, it's exposed to the sun all day, making a heavenly
spot to bask in the precious warmth with a local brew.

Cocktail Bars

*Years before craft cocktails went mainstream,
Vancouver was punching above its weight with some
of the most exciting mixology on the continent. And
today, the local scene is bigger and better than ever.*

CANTINA 189

**Map 2; 324 W Hastings Street, Gastown; ///crab.backup.dove;
www.cantina189.com**

It's dark, it's tiny, and when the room is full and the DJ is behind the
decks, it's gonna get loud. But none of that should put you off this
charming Mexican-themed watering hole. Cocktails stay on brand
with tequila and mezcal, combining familiar ingredients (citrus,
chili) with some "Excuse me?" surprises (charred corn, queso fresco).

BOTANIST

**Map 1; 1038 Canada Place, Coal Harbour; ///accusing.types.stays;
www.botanistrestaurant.com**

If any Vancouver bar asks you to expect the unexpected, this is it.
This self-described "cocktail lab" has won loads of awards (including
a place on Canada's top 10 bars list) not only because its drinks are
excellent, but because they look and taste like nothing you've had

before. Don't believe us? Name somewhere else you'd find a cocktail like Candy Cap Magic. It comes atop a bed of moss inside a lantern, which releases a dramatic cloud of dry ice when you open it.

» Don't leave without ordering a glass of B.C. grapes from Botanist's ever-changing, always-great list of sustainable and organic wines.

PIDGIN

Map 2; 350 Carrall Street, Gastown; ///spelled.exhales.crest; www.pidginvancouver.com

Vancouverites have a thing for Asian/Pacific Northwest fusion (hey, that's the city in a nutshell), and Pidgin plays with that concept more intriguingly than most. Case in point: the One Eyed Samurai, which features sake and watermelon-infused tequila. Cocktail connoisseurs also love the special extra touches, like Kodama ice – made locally and renowned for its clarity and impossibly clean flavor.

Next door to Slim's BBQ in Mount Pleasant is a storefront with the name "Zottenberg & Sons Accounting" on the window and an unmanned office inside. It's not what you think (really, it's not). Inside you'll find Key Party *(www.narrowgroup.ca)*, an "open secret" lounge done up to look like a 1970s rumpus room. In case the grown-up party vibe isn't explicit enough, cocktails have names like Pearl Necklace and Slippery When Wet. You've been warned.

Liked by the locals

"Vancouverites make their own fun, especially in their cocktail scene. It's a city where the bartenders ask, 'What if?' and let innovation reign."

OLIVIA POVARCHOOK, AWARD-WINNING
VANCOUVER BARTENDER

BAO BEI

Map 2; 163 Keefer Street, Chinatown; ///cuter.remake,examples;
www.bao-bei.ca

Way back in 2010, this impossibly chic Chinese brasserie single-
handedly rejuvenated the city's Chinatown. Hip restaurants and bars
have been packing 'em in ever since, thanks to Bao Bei's hugely
popular and dangerously gulpable black-tea based Nai Nai Punch.
» Don't leave without sampling at least a few dishes from the food
menu – the dumplings are especially good.

STRAIGHT & MARROW

Map 5; 1869 Powell Street, East Van; ///owls.steers.shock;
www.straightandmarrow.com

Vegan or vegetarian? You might want to sit this one out. Straight &
Marrow is renowned for its meat-heavy menu, which extends to the
house cocktail: a mixture of marrow-infused brandy, red wine, citrus,
and beef stock. Even carnivores might be glad to hear that the rest
of the drinks list is meat free (though it's just as boozy and delicious).

THE DIAMOND

Map 2; 6 Powell Street, Gastown; ///dragon.underway.secures;
www.di6mond.com

Lots of bars try to look like an old-time speakeasy, but The Diamond's
vintage vibe is legit. Housed in a building that dates back to the late
1800s, it's where couples come to raise an antique glass in a sultry,
candlelit start to the weekend.

WEST 2ND AVENUE

**Pizza and a pint at
R&B BREWING**

One of East Van's OG
microbreweries, this joint
has a taproom and a
restaurant serving a pizza
and a pint for $20.

③ EAST 4TH AVENUE

**Fill it up at
BRASSNECK**

This tasting room is always
lively, with 12 taps pouring
everything from fruity sours
to heavy stouts. Grab a
growler to go; the bottle is
yours to keep.

②

EAST 6TH AVENUE

MAIN STREET

EAST 1ST AVENUE

EAST 2ND AVENUE

SCOTIA

STREET

COLUMBIA STREET

MANITOBA STREET

WEST 8TH AVENUE ① EAST 8TH AVENUE

MOUNT
PLEASANT

**Ease into it at
33 ACRES**

Start your beer pilgrimage
with this brewery's signature
33 Acres of Ocean. Made
with ingredients harvested
locally, the IPA has notes of
citrus and pine.

EAST BROADWAY

KINGSWAY

MAIN STREET

0 meters 200
0 yards 200

MAIN STREET

An afternoon beer-hopping in
Mount Pleasant

In the 1880s, Mount Pleasant was the ideal spot for the city's burgeoning breweries, with quality water supplied by Brewery Creek (go figure). And not much has changed. Today "Yeast Van," as it's affectionately known, is home to the city's booming craft beer scene, with dozens of indie microbreweries setting up shop in the area's former auto-repair shops and vacant warehouses. For craft beer lovers who'll take a hazy IPA over a bottle of Bud Light any day, this is the perfect place for an afternoon spent beer-hopping and sipping ice-cold pints.

4 Keep it flowing at RED TRUCK BREWING
This truck-themed brewery is a whole experience. The beers are carried in most pubs in town, so try one of the experimental batches.

*The **Dude Chilling Park** sign was originally installed as a prank, but now has official public art status in Vancouver.*

1. 33 Acres
15 W 8th Avenue;
www.33acresbrewing.com
///requested.swam.bench

2. Brassneck
2148 Main Street;
www.brassneck.ca
///race.prepared.magnum

3. R&B Brewing
54 E 4th Avenue;
www.randbbrewing.com
///piles.migrants.fees

4. Red Truck Brewing
295 E 1st Ave; www.red
truckbeer.com
///race.prepared.magnum

Dude Chilling Park
///strategy.servers.stuffy

SHOP

Vancouverites are a discerning bunch; you'll find locals scouting indie stores for vintage garms, hand-crafted homewares, and thrilling reads by up-and-coming authors.

Book Nooks

Come rain or shine, Vancouver's bookstores are a welcome escape from the outside world. Here, locals stop to pick up their next ripping yarn, fuel for fertile imaginations.

MCLEOD'S BOOKS

Map 1; 455 W Pender Street, Downtown;
///princes.spin.widgets; (604) 681-7654

It's full-on chaos at McLeod's. For more than 40 years, locals have been getting lost amid crammed ceiling-height shelves, teetering stacks of paperbacks, and overflowing boxes of uncategorized new arrivals. If you're looking for something specific, good luck.

THE PAPER HOUND

Map 2; 344 W Pender Street, Downtown;
///ballroom.nutrients.steamed; www.paperhound.ca

This is the sort of bookstore you thought existed only in "meet cute" moments in 1990s rom-coms. Small and charming, this place strikes just the right balance between tidy and chaotic, and is staffed by literature lovers who would happily talk all day about what's on the shelves. And what is on those shelves, you ask? Well, there's a bit of everything – the latest fiction, pre-loved classics, whimsical collections, and drop-dead gorgeous design volumes that you'll fall head over heels in love with. Whatever your type, you're sure to find "the one."

» Don't leave without visiting the store's cigarette-machine-turned-poetry-dispenser. Curated by the Dead Poet's Reading Series *(www. deadpoetslive.com)*, it spits out works by late, great versifiers.

E.C. RARE BOOKS

Map 2; 323 Cambie Street, Gastown;
///infants.covers.email; www.ecrarebooks.com

True to its name, this place specializes in hard-to-find books that collectors spend a lifetime seeking out. Meticulously organized shelves in hushed rooms are home to all sorts of treasures, from first-edition 19th-century poetry volumes to ultra scarce illustrated children's books that sell for thousands of dollars. We can but look.

Davie Village, B.C.'s foremost "Gayborhood," is home to Little Sister's Book & Art Emporium *(www.littlesisters.ca)*. This trail-blazing shop has been a cornerstone of Vancouver's LGBTQ2S+ community since the '80s, and it stocks a peerless selection of queer literature from around the world. But wait, there's more. This place is a one-stop shop for all the bedroom accessories that any adventurous adult could possibly desire, whatever their orientation.

Liked by the locals

"I love books and I love Vancouver bookstores. And I'm so grateful for the incredible community of booksellers in this city who also love them and support our local writers."

ANDREA WARNER,
VANCOUVER-BASED AUTHOR AND JOURNALIST

LUCKY'S BOOKS & COMICS
Map 4; 3972 Main Street, South Main;
///stunning.salon.grills; www.luckys.ca

Comic geeks, cosplayers, and Vancouver nerds in the know hit up this tiny Tardis of a store for its surprisingly vast selection of comics, graphic novels, and indy zines. But the offerings don't end there. This place is also a mecca for games, puzzles, Pokemon cards, and more.
» **Don't leave without** picking up a copy of Lucky's *Dunk* newspaper. Collectors will be glad to know that backdated issues are available.

VILLAGE BOOKS & COFFEE HOUSE
Map 6; #130, 12031 1st Avenue, Steveston;
///unravel.requires.policy; www.villagebooksandcoffee.ca

Welcoming, unpretentious, and perfectly in keeping with the small-town vibe of Steveston Village, Village Books & Coffee House is a quiet refuge. Readers come to browse secondhand books, latte in hand, as the sounds of Steveston Harbour filter in from outside.

MASSY BOOKS
Map 2; 229 E Georgia Street, Strathcona;
///hometown.patch.fillers; www.massybooks.com

This Indigenous-owned shop is a stalwart of the city's creative scene. As well as selling the usual new and secondhand finds, Massy champions small-press titles by up-and-coming Canadian writers. Shelves roll away for author readings, music performances, and other events, while the upstairs gallery displays works by local artists.

Home Touches

Apartment dressing in Vancouver leans toward minimalist, forward-thinking, and functional. Cool art, handy kitchenware, handpoured candles – as long as it's locally made, Vancouverites love it.

THE REGIONAL ASSEMBLY OF TEXT

Map 4; 3934 Main Street, Mount Pleasant;
///swim.romance.everyone; www.assemblyoftext.com

Step back in time (and typefaces) at this retro stationery store, which is punctuated with an array of old school desks, antique typewriters, and treat-yourself stationery. Font fans who know their sans serifs from their scripts and craft enthusiasts seeking materials for their next creative project flock here to score some swanky notepads, colored paper, stamps, and stickers.

HARLOW ATELIER

Map 4; 655 E 15th Avenue, East Van
///unfolds.research.fizzle; www.harlowskinco.com

Originally founded to provide natural and organic self-care goods, this adorable little boutique now serves up anything Vancouver's most socially conscious shoppers might need. Unique items include

Next door, Gluten Free Epicurean's Danish of the Day is a must try (Thursdays and Saturdays only).

ethically produced homewares, vegan cookbooks, environmentally friendly glass straws, and natural cleaning supplies for keeping your home spick and span.

OLD FAITHFUL SHOP

Map 2; 320 W Cordova Street, Gastown;
///tins.twisty.deduced; www.oldfaithfulshop.com

Functionality, simplicity, and beauty. These are the Japanese design fundamentals behind the timeless pieces found at Old Faithful Shop. This place is coveted by design-savvy locals for its stylish yet practical kitchenware – think temperature-controlled tea kettles, rice donabes, and rose-gold garden scissors (okay, perhaps not the most practical).

>> Don't leave without picking a pair of the Japanese tabi socks – the giza cotton and a segregated big toe give a delightful barefoot feel.

KIMPRINTS

Map 2; 41 Powell Street, Gastown
///person.imposes.churn; www.kimprints.com

Since 1984, the good people of Gastown have been sourcing art for their walls from Kim of Kimprints. Her charming shop is housed in the Hotel Europe, Vancouver's take on New York City's Flatiron Building – albeit a smaller and humbler version, of course. And the friendly vibes don't stop there. Whether you've come to browse original works by Vancouver artists like Ken Foster, or peruse quirky gift items, Kim warmly welcomes everyone who crosses the threshold.

WALRUS DESIGN INC

Map 4; 3408 Cambie Street, Mount Pleasant;
///truly.gums.abolish; www.shop.walrushome.com

Gorgeous ceramics, hand-poured candles, striking wall art, and ever-so-tasteful kids' toys (no plastic here, thank you), Walrus Design is a celebration of Canadian art and design. Every piece has a story to tell, as do co-owners Caroline Boquist and Daniel Kozlowski. In fact, the pair of them love nothing more than to chat away to their many customers, sharing their intimate knowledge of their city, its culture, and, of course, its cutting-edge design.

BARTER DESIGN

Map 4; 637 E 15th Avenue, East Van;
///discrepancy.nowadays.remover; www.barterdesign.ca

Small but perfectly formed, this place feels more like an exclusive art gallery than a shop. Exhibits include sculptural furniture pieces, lighting installations, and decorative glassware, all handcrafted by B.C. makers in clay, wood, wool, concrete, steel, and even beeswax.

Try it!
MAKE YOUR OWN

At Granville Island's Make It (*www.makevancouver.com*) you can create your own stylish homewares from scratch. Have fun with custom-printing, engraving, and embroidery.

THE MODERN BARTENDER

Map 2; 28 E Pender Street, Chinatown;

///vocals.players.wir; www.themodernbartender.com

No apartment is complete without a home bar for wowing friends with a round of martinis. Vancouver's budding mixologists head here for all their cocktail-making needs, and you should too. Shakers, jiggers, strainers, and spoons – the selection of barware is second to none.

PROVIDE HOME

Map 3; 1805 Fir Street, Armoury District;

///empires.tagging.ensemble; www.providehome.com

Catering to the tastes of top interior designers, architects, and design-enthusiasts, this contemporary boutique is all about celebrating internationally acclaimed Vancouver designers and brands. Stunning pieces by local favorites like Martha Sturdy, Brent Comber, Hinterland, and Lock & Mortice can all be found here.

MUCH & LITTLE

Map 4; 2543 Main Street, Mount Pleasant;

///aims.bars.saunas; www.muchandlittle.com

Owner Sarah Savoy keeps her stylish store well stocked with hand-selected one-of-a-kind goodies made by Indigenous, indie, and women-led local businesses. It's hard not to love the sculptural jewelry pieces, floral jumpsuits, and jacquard napped throws.

» Don't leave without taking a whiff of Brand & Iron's small-batch scented candles. We defy you not to buy at least one.

Street Style

Vancouver is a pretty casual city, but that doesn't mean that locals rock the same old, practical clothes – far from it. The city's street style is all about self-expression and shopping local whenever possible.

THE BLOCK

Map 2; 350 W Cordova Street, Gastown;
///crumble.quiet.combines; www.theblock.ca

As one of the first established fashion boutiques in Gastown, The Block has definitely been around the block and back. Its fashion-forward threads and array of comfortable footwear, leather bags, and statement accessories have been spotted on Vancouver's scenesters since the 1980s. Sure, they don't come cheap, but prices reflect their quality and craftsmanship. Go on, treat yourself.

HERSCHEL

Map 2; 347 Water Street, Gastown; ///tickets.payback.holidays;
www.herschel.ca

This Vancouver-based lifestyle brand can be found all over the world, but you need to check out its flagship Gastown location for a uniquely local experience. Part backpack shop, part community

For a bargain, check out the Herschel outlet at the McArthur Glen Designer Outlet, right by the airport.

hub, this store regularly hosts talks, artist-in-residence programs, creative workshops, and fun community events. Pop in for a bag and stay for a gig.

ONE OF A FEW

Map 2; 354 Water Street, Gastown; ///hedge.liquids.rots; www.oneofafew.com

On-brand with Vancouver's values, store owner Michelle Rizzardo has really embraced the idea of "slow fashion" here at One of a Few. Only a limited number of pieces in her carefully curated collection are made, each in a distinctive style. From dresses to jewelry, and even organic and herbal skin care, anything you buy here is sure to be one of only a few (well, the clue is in the name).

JOHN FLUEVOG SHOES

Map 2; 65 Water Street, Gastown;///above.ordinary.invite; www.fluevog.com

It may now be a globally recognized brand but Fluevog knows where it came from, and still dreams up a collection of wacky designs in its hometown of Vancouver. Wacky, you say? Picture daring bubblegum pink, knee-high boots, complete with corset-style laces, or a shoe styled after a swordfish (don't ask) and you get the idea. "Unique Soles for Unique Souls," as the Fluevog slogan goes.

» Don't leave without visiting the Fluezeum online, where you'll find archives of all of John Fluevog's past designs.

VESSI

Map 6; 4700 Kingsway #2175, Burnaby; ///sprinkle.wicket.recount;
www.ca.vessi.com

Sick and tired of soggy sneakers, three weather-weary Vancouverites created a totally waterproof sneaker that became a literal game-changer. Andy, Tony, and Mikaella were adamant that their sneakers be sustainably produced and wholly functional, carefully designing a shoe that keeps socks dry and feet sweat-free. Oh, and they look great too, proving that functionality and style needn't be mutually exclusive (not that Vancouverites need much convincing here). Vessi sneakers have since become something of a Vancouver style essential; stroll through the city's streets and you're sure to see plenty of locals happily strutting around in their Vessis with little to no regard for pesky puddles.

>> Don't leave without trying on a pair of Vessi waterproof gloves, which are made from the same breathable knit as the sneakers.

OAK + FORT

Map 2; 151 Water Street, Gastown;
///openings.erupted.stand; www.ca.oakandfort.com

Minimal, stylish, and affordable: these were the founding values of the fledgling Oak + Fort e-commerce site, set up by husband and wife team Arjuna and Min over a decade ago. Over the years, the brand's minimalist vibe, sleek and contemporary designs, and relatively affordable price tags proved to be a winning combination, with this brick-and-mortar store opening in 2010. Now, fashion-forward locals glide around this flagship store in search of chic everyday threads that are perfect for brunch with the gang. Think oversized sweaters, neutral tones, and faux leather pants. Not sure where to begin? Staff are super friendly and always on hand to offer style tips.

HILL'S OF KERRISDALE
Map 6; 2125 W 41st Avenue, Kerrisdale;
///oaks.compiled.haven; www.hillsofkerrisdale.com

A Westside institution since the 1920s, this multi-generational family business has been around longer than most Kerrisdale locals can remember. Sure, the vintage-inspired interiors are a nod to its past, but inside you'll find all the contemporary brands you could possibly desire – Citizens of Humanity, Dr. Martens, Levis, Birkenstock, Barbour, and Aritzia (we could go on). Everything is lovingly curated by siblings Ross and Nancy, who are the third generation to run the business. We challenge you to leave empty-handed.

Shh!

Known by only the savviest Vancouver fashionistas, the FX Fashion Exchange Building (www.fxfashionexchange.com) stands in an unassuming industrial area on the edge of Downtown. But don't let the location put you off – this place is worth the trip. Here you'll find an array of retailers, from big names to boutique pop-ups, all offering clothes, handbags, and shoes, and all at heavily reduced wholesale prices. Lines are usually out the door by 8am, so remember to set your alarm.

Vintage Gems

*Champions of sustainability, Vancouverites will choose
pre-loved over fast fashion and flatpack any day.
Have a rummage in these secondhand haunts and
bag a one-of-a-kind piece that doesn't cost the Earth.*

RELOVE FURNITURE

**Map 5; 286 Keefer Street, Strathcona; ///routines.gravy.nests;
www.relovefurniture.com**

Nestled away in the cool and quirky neighborhood of Strathcona,
this retro consignment store embodies the effortlessly cool vibes of
the community. Locals can't get enough of its bohemian wicker and
mid-century modern, popping in every other week to croon over the
latest pieces and longingly picture them in their apartments.

THE MAIN EXCHANGE

**Map 4; 3728 Main Street; South Main; ///fully.survivor.donation;
www.themainexchange.ca**

The more discerning vintage shopper will be happy to part with their
paycheck at this darling boutique of pre-loved fashion. Browse
owner Miranda's thoughtfully chosen collection of stylish pieces
in the hope of finding designer bargains and nearly new and

in-season Lululemon and Aritzia garms – the essential Vancouver wardrobe – without compromising on any environmental principles by forking out for new clothing. It's a true win-win situation.

MINE & YOURS

Map 1; 418 Davie Street, Yaletown; ///surreal.filer.fails;
www.mineandyours.com

Ever wondered what it would be like to shop the closets of the rich and famous? At Mine & Yours, dreams become a reality. Shop owner Courtney Watkins is incredibly well connected and procures many of the designer goodies (think Louis Vuitton, Gucci, Prada, Valentino) she sells in her couture shop from stars and celebrities.

CARRIAGE HOUSE

Map 2; 104 E Pender Street, Chinatown; ///ranted.thrones.edges;
www.carriagehouseinteriors.ca

Luxe homeware and one-of-a-kind artworks stacked floor to ceiling are the name of the game at this consignment store. Shoppers come here for the quality and sheer variety of styles. But they're not the only ones. This place is also a favorite among set designers searching for that perfect prop for the silver screen; *Fifty Shades of Grey, Night at the Museum,* and *Mission Impossible* all featured a Carriage House piece in a starring role.

» Don't leave without booking a staging and home design consultation. These guys really know their stuff, and they'd love nothing more than to help beautify your home (for a fee, of course).

HEY JUDE

Map 2; 315 Abbott Street, Gastown; ///backs.packing.dips;
www.heyjudeshop.com

Whether you're rummaging this store's vintage racks or browsing its sustainably produced fashion, you'll want to make a lifelong commitment to anything you buy here. And that's exactly what Hey Jude's sustainable, "shop slow" ethos is all about.

» Don't leave without visiting nearby Beat Street Records for old and new vinyl, art supplies, and music memorabilia.

COLLECTIVE WILL

Map 2; #1400–207 W Hastings Street, Gastown;
///plug.lamp.marginal; www.shopcollectivewill.com

Owner and award-winning fashion blogger Randa Salloum skims the racks of local thrift stores so you don't have to, styling ready-to-wear looks that breathe life into your closet. Her motivation? To inspire shoppers to ditch fast fashion and love what's already out there. The fact that her community-minded shop also feels more like an exclusive design studio than a stuffy thrift store is a bonus, really.

HUNTER & HARE

Map 2; 227 Union Street, Strathcona; ///says.voted.tenders;
www.hunterandhare.com

With its carefully chosen selection of women's clothing, this community consignment store is a fashion mood board come to life. Supersoft cashmere, chunky knits, pre-loved leather jackets, and mom jeans

Check out the nearby Eastside Flea, where artisan, vintage, and food vendors gather for massive markets.

galore: racks abound with the kind of timeless apparel your closet simply craves, and the garments are so on trend you really won't believe they're secondhand.

MINTAGE MALL

Map 4; 245 E Broadway, Mount Pleasant;
//loving.standing.reserve; www.mintage-mall.business.site

We can't talk about Vancouver's vintage scene and not mention Mintage Mall, a labyrinthine marketplace housing various vintage retailers. Weekends in the mall are particularly busy, with teenagers eyeing up '90s bomber jackets in Remixed Vintage and students trying on Low Life's rock band tees. And our favorite concession? It's hard to resist the Y2K-inspired jewelry by Oomph (with its colorful pom-poms, beads, and plastic dinosaurs). The mall even has an in-house café for when you need a post-shopping pick-me-up.

F AS IN FRANK

Map 4; 2425 Main Street, Mount Pleasant; ///hopeless.exhale.itself;
www.fasinfrankvintage.com

F as in Frank is an all-gender streetwear lover's paradise, teeming with secondhand Levis, crewnecks, Nike deadstock, leather and hand-cropped Harley Davidson tees. Be sure to wander into the back corner of the store where you'll find an unassuming room offering absolute steals, sometimes even a whole bag full of pre-loved clothes for as little as $10. We do love a bargain.

Outdoor Gear

Mountains, forests, beaches, and ocean – why wouldn't you want to explore Vancouver's great outdoors? Get among it as the locals do, just make sure you're decked out in the right gear.

ARC'TERYX

Map 1; 813 Burrard Street, Downtown; ///shaver.copies.turkey; www.arcteryx.com

A familiar sight to many, this flagship store's ultra-modern, angular facade is a nod to B.C.'s jagged North Shore Mountains (it's no substitute for the original, of course, but it's a nod nonetheless). And the nature-inspired design continues inside, too. The place is a vision in wood and stone, with natural color palettes that make

Try it!
TIME TO PLAY

Rock climbing, skating, or a game of drop-in basketball – sports fans, you'll appreciate the chance to play at the Richmond Olympic Oval, which hosted long-track skating events in the 2010 Winter Games.

It's worth visiting the Arc'teryx Outlet in North Vancouver for some last-chance deals on outdoor gear.

it easy to imagine the reams of outdoorsy garms and gear lining the store's shelves serving you well in their intended setting – the great outdoors.

SPORTS JUNKIES

Map 4; 102 W Broadway, Mount Pleasant;
///reds.girder.tubes; www.sportsjunkies.com

Locals like to keep this one to themselves, but we're happy to let you in on the secret. Sports Junkies carries new, discontinued, and pre-loved sportswear, all at heavily discounted prices. If you're willing to put in the time to rummage, your wallet will thank you later.

LULULEMON

Map 3; 2101 W 4th Avenue, Kitsilano;
///boxer.national.solids; www.shop.lululemon.com

Yes, you can shop for Lululemon online, or anywhere in the world for that matter, but why not see where it all started at the OG Lulu? Here you'll find all the usual activewear apparel, but what makes this place really special is its brand nostalgia (yup, it's a thing), which harks back to Lululemon's early days. Look out for a retro auto-repair sign that displays inspiring yogi slogans like "Yoga, Run, Party," skateboard stickers covering vintage cabinets, and a mural by local artist Paige Bowman depicting iconic Vancouver city scenes.

» **Don't leave without** grabbing a refreshing drink from the store's dedicated kombucha tap (we kid you not).

MEC

Map 4; 111 E 2nd Avenue, Olympic Village;
///ocean.grocers.surveyed; www.mec.ca

When planning their next camping trip, locals' first port of call is specialist equipment store MEC. Once they've pitched their tent, they can sleep safe in the knowledge that it came from a company that operates sustainably to protect the environment they so love to explore.

DUER

Map 3; 1757 W 4th Avenue, Kitsilano; ///rents.twists.brother;
www.duer.ca

Fast becoming another Vancouver household name, DUER prides itself on creating the most comfortable pants ever. And the locals are obsessed. DUER's line of denim, joggers, and work pants are made from recycled materials (very Vancouver) and offer the ultimate stretch for comfort and style so you can hit the trail straight from the office.

>> Don't leave without attempting a lunge in a pair of the performance denim pants. You'll be shocked at the stretch in these miracle jeans.

TAIGA WORKS

Map 6; 3454 Bridgeway Street, East Van;
///recruited.bashed.partners; www.taigaworks.com

Don't be put off by the unassuming factory and industrial setting of this one. Aimed primarily at folks who work outdoors (Canadian winters are no joke), this is the place to pick up quality outdoor gear. Think cozy down jackets, thermals, and ultra-waterproof trousers.

Liked by the locals

"Vancouver's motto, 'There
is no such thing as bad weather,
only bad gear', holds true. With
the city being a haven of technical
gear, there really is no excuse
not to get out there!"

ALI CHAPKIN,
LOCAL OUTDOOR ENTHUSIAST

A morning shopping on
Main Street

An array of vintage stores, quirky bookstores, and one-of-a kind independent boutiques line the Main Street corridor, making it the perfect stomping ground for locals craving some retail therapy. And, in true Vancouver style, these stores champion local designers and makers by selling handcrafted, sustainably produced goods. Tote bag at the ready – we defy you to leave Main Street empty-handed.

1. F as in Frank
2425 Main Street; www.
fasinfrankvintage.com
///hopeless.exhale.itself

2. Urban Source
3126 Main Street;
www.urban-source.ca
///stored.nods.molars

3. Welk's General Store
3511 Main Street;
www.welks.ca
///goggles.silver.swept

4. Vancouver Special
3612 Main Street;
www.shop.vanspecial.com
///flipper.bands.union

5. Front & Company
3772 Main Street; www.
frontandcompany.com
///coached.plunge.easy

6. Lucky's Books & Comics
3972 Main Street;
www.luckys.ca
///stunning.salon.grills

Neptoon Records
///issues.solution.tedious

CAMBIE STREET

WEST 16TH AVEN

WEST 20TH AVEN

WEST KING EDWARD AVE

0 meters 250
0 yards 250

1 Relive your youth at
F AS IN FRANK

Enjoy a dose of nostalgia by
trying on vintage hockey
jerseys and 1990s band tees
at this lovingly curated shop.

WEST BROADWAY

EAST BROADWAY

QUEBEC STREET

MAIN STREET

WEST 12TH AVENUE

EAST 12TH AVENUE

KINGSWAY

Get crafty at
URBAN SOURCE

Feeling inspired? You
definitely will be after a visit to
Urban Source, where crafty
Vancouverites come to pick
up all sorts of supplies for their
next creative project.

2

EAST 15TH AVENUE

EAST 16TH AVENUE

MAIN STREET

Neptoon Records *has
been open since 1981,
making it Vancouver's
oldest independent
record store.*

Pop into
WELK'S GENERAL STORE

Grab a basket at the door of this upscale
general store. Welk's sells quality goods
for everyday living. Candles, cookware,
and cocktail ingredients – it's all here.

3

Style your home at
VANCOUVER SPECIAL

Locals can't resist the minimalist ceramic
goods here, and you won't be able to either.

4

EAST 21ST AVENUE

5 ### Rummage the racks at
FRONT & COMPANY

MAIN ST

Get your geek on at
LUCKY'S BOOKS & COMICS

End your tour flicking through Lucky's extensive
collection of comic books and graphic novels.

Quality consignment clothing and quirky gifts
galore; Front & Company is where you'll find that
special something you never knew you needed.

6

EAST KING EDWARD AVENUE

ARTS & CULTURE

Known as Hollywood North, Vancouver has a thriving arts and culture scene. Creative spaces allow imaginations to run free, and the whole city is a canvas for public art.

City History

From First Nations settlement to major fishing center and beyond, Vancouver sure has a rich history. Uncover the story of the city's evolution at these important spots.

MUSQUEAM CULTURAL CENTRE

Map 6; 4000 Musqueam Avenue, Dunbar-Southlands;
///founding.shunts.writing; www.musqueam.bc.ca

Vancouver sits on the traditional territories of three local First Nations: the Musqueam, Squamish, and Tsleil-Waututh. These communities were long marginalized – a part of Vancouver's past that the city continues to wrestle with – but places like the Musqueam Cultural Centre are working hard to keep their legacy alive. Expect displays of everything from historical objects to works of contemporary art.

ROEDDE HOUSE MUSEUM

Map 3; 1415 Barclay Street, West End; ///released.dreamer.badly;
www.roeddehouse.org

When German couple Gustav and Matilda Roedde moved here in 1888, Vancouver had only officially been a city for two years. It's fair to say that life back then was pretty rustic. But the Roeddes' pioneering spirit saw them establish the city's first bookbinding business, and make enough money to build this house. Today featuring the addition of some luxury touches (water, electricity), it acts as a fascinating time capsule from the city's first urban settlers.

CHINESE CANADIAN MUSEUM
Map 2; 51 E Pender Street, Chinatown; ///veered.solar.risks; www.chinesecanadianmuseum.ca

With nearly 20 per cent of the city's population having Chinese ancestry, Chinese culture is a big part of Vancouver's identity. And this museum is here to celebrate that. It takes a personal look at the history of the city's Chinatown, sharing local people's memories of things like food and family businesses. Visitors are invited to add their own stories to the collection, making it a cool living space that's always changing.

» **Don't leave without** strolling through the delightful Dr. Sun Yat-Sen Classical Chinese Garden *(p117)* across the street.

If you're going to the beach at Jericho, stop in to see the Old Hastings Mill Store Museum *(https://hastingsmillmuseum.ca)*. This small wooden structure may not look like much, but it's actually the city's oldest building. Moved to Point Grey in 1931, it originally stood in Gastown as a store and social hub. Nowadays it's full of fascinating historical curios, including a chair saved from the 1886 Great Vancouver Fire.

GULF OF GEORGIA CANNERY
Map 6; 12138 4th Avenue, Steveston;
///terminology.observer.uniforms; https://gulfofgeorgiacannery.org

A field trip here is a much-loved rite of passage for many of the city's elementary school kids. Dedicated to the history of fishing – one of Vancouver's mainstay industries since the late 19th century – the museum's warts-and-all exhibits outline the tough working conditions and will fill you with your own sense of childlike awe.

» Don't leave without visiting nearby Britannia Shipyards, a cluster of buildings that tell the stories of the European, First Nations, Chinese, and Japanese communities during the 19th-century fishing boom.

MUSEUM OF VANCOUVER
Map 3; 1100 Chestnut Street, Kitsilano; ///flasks.twin.cover;
https://museumofvancouver.ca

Where better to learn about the history of Vancouver than at the city's oldest museum? The exhibitions here trace life through the decades, highlighting generational changes with displays of clothing, home

Try it!
WALK IN THE PARK

Sign up for a walk with Talaysay Tours (*www.talaysay.com*) and explore the forested trails of Stanley Park through the eyes of a First Nations guide – it'll make you appreciate nature in an all-new way.

The museum shares an entrance with the H.R. MacMillan Space Centre, so you can hit both in one visit.

appliances, and more. Our favorite is the 1960s exhibit, which shows how the hippie-dippie neighborhood of Kitsilano championed the city's flower power scene.

THE MARINE BUILDING

Map 1; 355 Burrard Street, Coal Harbour; ///parts.travel.insects; (604) 893-3248

Vancouver might be known nowadays as the "City of Glass," but its postcard-perfect skyline hasn't always been dominated by glittering minimalist towers. In fact, one of the earliest structures to hold bragging rights as the city's tallest building was this sublime Art Deco skyscraper. Equally opulent inside and out, it's beloved by awestruck architecture students. Join them in poring over the building's intricate features, including inlaid-wood elevator interiors and gleaming bronze shells and seahorses.

BURNABY VILLAGE MUSEUM

Map 6; 6501 Deer Lake Avenue, Edmonds; ///farmland.premises.aware; www.burnabyvillagemuseum.ca

With its historical buildings and staff dressed in period clothes, this huge (and free) open-air museum offers an immersive taste of pioneer life in British Columbia in the 1920s. Embrace the experience by ordering sweet treats from an old-fashioned ice-cream parlor, watching a demonstration at Wagner's Blacksmith Shop, and taking a class at the traditional schoolhouse.

Favorite Museums

It's not all hiking and snowsports here, you know. Away from the mountains, Vancouverites love nothing better than soaking up some culture at the city's incredible array of museums and galleries.

MUSEUM OF ANTHROPOLOGY

Map 6; 6393 NW Marine Drive, University of British Columbia; ///either.calls.snapping; www.moa.ubc.ca

Not only does this museum house an incredible collection of art by Northwest Coast First Nations, but it's also home to thousands of everyday and ceremonial objects from communities around the world. You could easily spend a whole day (or more) perusing the beautiful totem poles, masks, canoes, baskets, and pots. Comfy shoes are a must.

VANCOUVER ART GALLERY

Map 1; 50 Hornby Street, Downtown; ///serious.food.bouncing; www.vanartgallery.bc.ca

Before browsing the boutiques of Robson Street, set aside the morning to check out the latest exhibitions at the VAG (as locals call it). Its expertly curated art shows change regularly, so you never know quite what you might find. It's just as likely to be a priceless set of paintings by a giant of international art as an obscure sculpture collection by a little-known local artist.

» **Don't leave without** stopping for a bite or a cocktail at the in-house 1931 Gallery Bistro *(p76)*.

THE POLYGON GALLERY

Map 6; 101 Carrie Cates Court, Lower Lonsdale, North Vancouver;
///punch.workforce.lavender; www.thepolygon.ca

With its sharply angled roof and all-glass street façade, the Polygon looks pretty serious from the outside. Inside, though, fun and inclusivity are the name of the game, with a by-donation admission policy, weekend kids' programing, and rotating exhibits of contemporary Canadian photography that are as playful as they are thought-provoking.

DR. SUN YAT-SEN CLASSICAL CHINESE GARDEN

Map 2; 578 Carrall Street, Chinatown; ///bikers.match.models;
www.vancouverchinesegarden.com

In recent years, historic Chinatown has been making headlines for all the wrong reasons (homelessness, crime, gentrification wars). But this beautiful Ming Dynasty-style garden remains an oasis of calm in the midst of urban turbulence. Okay, it's not technically a museum, but it regularly hosts art exhibitions and other cultural events inside the garden's traditional Chinese buildings.

Solo, Pair, Crowd

Looking for a space for a fun group outing? Or an hour or two of quiet contemplation? Vancouver has a museum for you.

FLYING SOLO
Wander through history
Discover the incredible past of one of Vancouver's most historic neighborhoods with Chinatown Storytelling Centre's immersive self-guided tour.

IN A PAIR
Be partners in crime
Despite its dry name, the Vancouver Police Museum & Archives is actually a lot of fun. Learn about unsolved murders or explore a former autopsy suite – a perfect excuse to hold your date that little bit closer.

FOR A CROWD
Rural outfitters
The next best thing to time travel, London Heritage Farm offers an insight into agricultural life in the early 1900s. Which one of you is best at working an old-fashioned butter churn? Find out here.

BEATY BIODIVERSITY MUSEUM

**Map 6; 2212 Main Mall, University of British Columbia;
///ambition.gathers.busy; www.beatymuseum.ubc.ca**

Ever wondered just how big a blue whale really is? The answer is
waiting at this shrine to natural history. Alongside the 85-ft (26-m)
whale skeleton in the atrium, the collection includes more than two
million specimens, ranging from birds to insects to plants.

» Don't leave without watching a screening of *Raising Big Blue*, a
documentary about how the blue whale was transported to the museum.

BILL REID GALLERY OF NORTHWEST COAST ART

**Map 1; 639 Hornby Street, Downtown; ///areas.moguls.sending;
www.billreidgallery.ca**

The late Bill Reid spent most of his life in Vancouver and played a huge
role in introducing the masses to Northwest Coast Indigenous art. This
small but beautiful space continues his mission with rotating exhibitions and also displays many of Reid's own sculptures and carvings.

VANCOUVER MARITIME MUSEUM

**Map 3; 1905 Ogden Avenue, Vanier Park; ///hands.trucked.desire;
www.vanmaritime.com**

Covering the history of all things maritime, the VMM celebrates the
city's ties to the sea. That includes a full-size boat you can board and
explore, as well as exhibits on important events like the founding of
Greenpeace in the cafés of neighboring Kitsilano.

Art Spaces

Vancouver has a creative soul, inspired by its beautiful natural surroundings. The art community here is warm and welcoming, with numerous spaces where people come together to make and share.

SKWACHÀYS LODGE

Map 2; 31 W Pender Street, Downtown;
///calculating.outgoing.directly; https://skwachays.com

Not only is Skwachàys Canada's first Indigenous arts hotel – complete with its own gallery – but it also provides housing and studios to 24 Indigenous artists-in-residence. Plus, the whole place is run as a self-sustaining social enterprise that ensures artists are paid a fair price for their work (which ranges from sculptures and fine art to clothing and jewelry). It's about as inspirational as an art space can get.

PARKER STREET STUDIOS

Map 5; 1000 Parker Street, East Van; ///booklet.nappy.nearly;
www.parkerartsalon.com

Stepping into Parker Street Studios is like falling down the rabbit hole. A complex maze of four floors filled with artists, makers, and creative studios, it's a wonderland of art, photography, sculpture, furniture, home accessories, plants, installations, and more. Oh, and it's also the main site for the annual Eastside Culture Crawl – a beloved local event that draws thousands here every November.

» **Don't leave without** venturing around the back of the building by the train tracks to see an array of graffiti art by local artists.

ROUNDHOUSE COMMUNITY ARTS & RECREATION CENTRE

Map 1; 181 Roundhouse Mews, Yaletown; ///soils.landmark.forks; www.roundhouse.ca

Rainy weather getting you down? Brighten your day with a trip to the Roundhouse. In any given week, you might catch an operatic Zimbabwean art installation, a one-man show about oppression in Argentina, or a concert of traditional Hawaiian music. It's fantastically varied, and that's why we love it.

EMILY CARR UNIVERSITY OF ART + DESIGN GALLERIES

Map 4; 520 E 1st Avenue, East Van; ///armrest.clues.remove; https://libby.ecuad.ca

Canada's top university for art and design, ECU is a hive of creativity. And that's as true of its public galleries as it is of its classrooms. Sketchbook-carrying artists find inspiration in rotating temporary exhibitions, while students wow their friends and family at the latest school shows. Even the campus itself is thought-provoking, with a huge outdoor "Urban Screen" displaying contemporary digital works.

DALBERGIA WOOD AND FINE OBJECTS
Map 3; 1339 Railspur Alley, Granville Island; ///blame.punchy.skater; https://granvilleisland.com

Working with natural materials and inspired by the city's cultures and artistic traditions, Venezuelan-born Federico Mendez-Castro takes all of Vancouver's best parts and turns them into art. He leaves the entire front of his studio open to passersby, inviting them to watch him sculpt or simply stop for a conversation. You won't regret saying hi.

THE PENDULUM GALLERY
Map 1; 885 W Georgia Street, Downtown; ///fatter.coder.drew; www.pendulumgallery.bc.ca

Housed in the bustling public atrium of the HSBC Canada building, the Pendulum Gallery brightens what would otherwise be a boring office space. Art-loving 9–5ers stop by at lunch to admire everything from oil paintings of flowers to sustainability-inspired installations.

THE UBC ARTS & CULTURE DISTRICT
Map 6; 1866 Main Mall, UBC Campus; ///helpers.performs.spray; www.arts.ubc.ca/arts-culture

Way out at Vancouver's westernmost point, the UBC campus is its own little city within a city. It's even got a dedicated Arts & Culture District, where students and scholars showcase their talents. Head here to discover future stars of art, music, theater, opera, and film.

» Don't leave without chatting to the super-helpful staff at the UBC Welcome Centre; they're always happy to help visitors make plans.

Liked by the locals

"As a newcomer to Vancouver, I was impressed to find artists of every kind in every corner of the city. Art is everywhere; it's accessible, tells the vital stories of First Nations and, importantly, encourages curiosity."

JASMIN FEDDER, VFX COMPOSITOR

On Stage and Screen

Here in Hollywood North, creative Vancouverites make blockbusters by day and catch shows by night. It's a quality-over-quantity scene, with a diverse mix of cinemas and theaters offering an entertainment fix.

VIFF CENTRE

Map 1; 1181 Seymour Street, Downtown; ///benched.whites.boating; https://viff.org

Art house lovers and documentary geeks, rejoice. If you're looking for unique movies you won't see anywhere else, this is where you'll find them. The Vancouver International Film Festival (VIFF) presents a stacked program of screenings here each fall, but you can catch cross-genre indie movies and other major film fests year-round.

ARTS CLUB THEATRE COMPANY

Map 3; 1585 Johnson Street, Fairview; ///hotdog.opinion.power; https://artsclub.com

What's the perfect end to a day spent noshing on market treats and browsing endless art shops on Granville Island? Watching a performance at the Arts Club's Granville Island Stage, of course.

One of three nonprofit venues run by the largest theater club in the city, its shows are anything but predictable – past performances have spanned everything from *The Sound of Music* to artistic takes on niche local controversies.

QUEEN ELIZABETH THEATRE

Map 1; 630 Hamilton Street, Downtown; ///encoded.table.steamed; https://vancouvercivictheatres.com

With its crimson seats, ornate ceiling design and glitzy chandeliers, the Queen Elizabeth Theatre will make you feel like royalty. But the setting is just a delightful bonus. This is Vancouver's leading entertainment venue, where big-name musicians, comedians, and Broadway productions take to the stage almost every night of the week. For a more local touch, check out a Ballet BC show.

» Don't leave without seeing what's on at the Vancouver Playhouse – the theater's cozy little sister venue in the same building.

VANCOUVER MEN'S CHORUS

Map 1; 600 Hamilton Street, Downtown; ///spite.clothed.hushed; www.vancouvermenschorus.ca

This is choir, but queer – and way more fun. Canada's first-ever gay chorus makes stages sparkle across the city. Add some ho-ho-ho into the holidays with the choir's well-loved seasonal show at the Vancouver Playhouse in December, and look out for the annual drag extravaganza during Pride in July, "where the heels are high but the falsettos are higher."

CINEMATHEQUE

Map 1; 1131 Howe Street, Downtown; ///dean.ground.dwarves;
https://thecinematheque.ca

Cannes meets Vancouver at the Cinematheque, where the avant-garde and experimental international film scene is brought to local screens. Galvanizing a niche community of dedicated, die-hard regulars, it's the go-to spot for film festivals and a place where post-screening debates in the lobby are welcome.

THE RIO

Map 5; 1660 E Broadway, East Van; ///call.hobbies.goals;
https://riotheatre.ca

Steeped in eclectic, left-field pop culture, the Rio is a beloved institution. So much so, in fact, that when it came under threat of demolition by new developers (a classic Vancouver conundrum), the

In the literal shadow of the larger Orpheum Theatre sits the effortlessly cool The Annex (*https://vancouvercivictheatres.com*), a cabaret-style venue that screams hepcat jazz à la 1950. Here you can see a wide range of dance and musical performances, all making the most of the venue's mind-blowing acoustics. When the music starts, you'll physically feel the sounds of orchestras, brass bands, and operatic vibratos reverberating off the cherry-red curtained walls.

city banded together and fundraised the money to save it. Rescuing the esteemed cinema was a huge win for East Van locals and film geeks everywhere — and especially for local celeb Ryan Reynolds, who famously tweeted that he plans to be buried there one day.

FIREHALL ARTS CENTRE

Map 2; 280 E Cordova Street, East Van; //backup.decades.transmit; https://firehallartscentre.ca

The Firehall takes intimate to a whole new level, with seating virtually integrated into its minimalist stage. Committed to inclusive access for underrepresented performers, the theater actively uplifts Indigenous and culturally diverse creatives. In short: it's a great place to see interdisciplinary performance art with a social justice edge.

» Don't leave without popping by the Firehall's in-house art gallery, which hosts revolving displays of visual works by local artists.

SCOTIABANK DANCE CENTRE

Map 1; 677 Davie Street, Downtown; ///slime.spotted.electric; https://thedancecentre.ca

Let your imagination flow with the music and movement at the Scotiabank Dance Centre. Whether you're into flamenco, ballet, hip-hop, contemporary dance, or vogueing, this is where you'll see Vancouver's best movers and shakers. And if you're not satisfied treating dance as a spectator sport, get in on the action at a free or pay-what-you-can workshop.

Public Art

Ever since the Vancouver Mural Festival stepped onto the scene in 2016, the city's once-barren walls have been splashed in color, brightening up the city on even the rainiest of days.

DIGITAL ORCA

Map 1; 1055 Canada Place, Coal Harbour; ///vanish.crunchy.newest

Everyone hopes to see a killer whale leaping from the Pacific but – we hate to break it to you – it's pretty rare to have a real-life *Free Willy* experience. So check out the next best thing: a pixelated orca at the Vancouver Convention Centre, designed by beloved local author and artist, Douglas Coupland. It looks like it's jumping straight from a 1980s video game and into the city-side sea.

Try it!
TAKE A TOUR

Check out the Vancouver Mural Tour website *(https://vancouvermurals.ca)* for four self-guided tours through various eastside neighborhoods. It's a great way to explore where the locals live.

THE WALL FOR WOMEN

Map 1; 655 Burrard Street, Downtown; ///shark.thigh.observes

The Wall for Women isn't just an art piece – it's a powerful message. This towering mural depicts a 42-ft- (13-m-) tall female figure, who represents a survivor of domestic abuse. The subject matter isn't just implied symbolically. Hidden among the artwork's Eastern European motifs (a trademark of the artist, Vancouver-raised Ola Volo) are six integrated QR codes. Scan each in turn to learn more about domestic abuse and donate to a local women's housing project. (Hint: they're largely found in the woman's pant legs and in the heel of her shoe.)

» Don't leave without wandering over to the pink, basketball-inspired alley known as "Alley-Oop" at 668 W Hastings Street. It's a popular setting for music videos and pop-up street parties.

A-MAZE-ING LAUGHTER

Map 3; 1800 Morton Avenue, West End;
///widget.siblings.symphony

One of Vancouver's most recognizable sculpture installations, these 14 shirtless giants are guaranteed to make you LOL. Each with their own unique, goofy smile, the A-maze-ing Laughter figures weren't meant to stay in the city for more than a couple of years. But locals became so attached to the silly statues by Chinese artist Yue Minjun that Vancouver billionaire and Lululemon founder Chip Wilson stepped in and bought them, giving them a permanent home in English Bay's Morton Park. Now the city's residents always have something to smile about.

GIANTS

Map 3; 1415 Johnston Street, Fairview; ///uniform.annoys.acute

We love it when ugly industrial infrastructure gets a glow-up. Take the Giants at Granville Island. These six, 70-ft (21-m) concrete silo towers used to blend into the dull gray of a rainy day. Then along came Brazilian twins Gustavo and Otavio Pandolfo, who painted the silos into characters with loud outfits and unimpressed smiles. Today they're among the city's most photogenic features.

THE MATRIARCH

Map 4; 2301 Main Street, Mount Pleasant; ///reader.tweaked.basin

Mount Pleasant is overflowing with outdoor murals, but few works are as impactful as *The Matriarch* by Siobhan Joseph of the Squamish First Nation. With her hands raised, the Matriarch simultaneously shows gratitude for the land and welcomes others onto it – a powerful gesture, as the city is situated on the Squamish Nation's traditional territory. Take note of her dress, which is colored red to raise awareness about missing and murdered Indigenous women in Canada.

EAST VANCOUVER COMMUNITY MURAL

Map 5; 1497 Adanac Street, East Van; ///factory.mandates.shiver

After grabbing a scoop of gelato at La Casa Gelata, head over to the nearby East Van Community Mural. This crowdfunded artistic celebration of East Van's cycling obsession was created by artists Jeff Dywelska and Kamila Grygorczyk. Smartly located along the

Head to Clark Drive and 6th Avenue to see the East Van Cross – a similarly iconic work by Ken Lum.

neighborhood's main bike drag, Adanac Street, it's also a great spot to watch Vancouver's pedal-powered Autobahn in action.

THE SPINNING CHANDELIER

Map 1; Beach Avenue, Yaletown; ///bunks.declines.chose

Designed by Rodney Graham, this massive, kinetic crystal chandelier is suspended in the underbelly of the Granville Street Bridge. As might be expected of such a glitzy statement piece, the light fixture comes with some drama. Made from 600 faux crystals, and coming with a hefty $4.8 million price tag (footed by a local luxury real estate developer), the work has been criticized as a display of opulence in a city facing a housing crisis. It's one of Vancouver's most controversial art installations.

» Don't leave without seeing the lights in action: this mammoth chandelier glitters, twirls, and dances daily at 12pm, 4pm, and 9pm.

217.5 ARC X 13

Map 3; 1204 Beach Avenue, West End; ///reported.owes.rush

"Sunset at the metal ribs, see you there," is a message frequently sent by Vancouverites linking up with friends. Designed by French artist Bernar Venet and reminiscent of a whale's ribcage, this iconic Sunset Beach landmark isn't a "don't touch the art" kind of piece – feel free to use its bones as a jungle gym, a place to string a hammock, or as a prop for an epic sunset photo.

An afternoon exploring
Indigenous Art Downtown

First Nations art is a huge part of city life, and nowhere is this more evident than in Downtown. Here, sculptures, totem poles, and vibrant murals breathe life into public spaces and Indigenous-owned galleries display stunning artworks. A walk through the area reveals the original stories of the city, as told by the Musqueam, Squamish, and Tsleil-Waututh artists whose ancestors lived here.

1. Skwachàys Lodge
31 W Pender Street; www.skwachays.com/art-gallery
///calculating.outgoing.directly

2. Coastal Peoples Fine Arts Gallery
332 Water Street, Unit 200;
www.coastalpeoples.com
///learn.spiking.hang

3. Cathedral Square
566 Richards Street
///glades.tools.disclose

4. Snékwem Lane
531 Granville Street
///dodges.palms.punchy

5. Bill Reid Gallery
639 Hornby Street;
www.billreidgallery.ca
///areas.moguls.sending

6. The Winds and Waters Will Always Call Us Home
999 Canada Place
///mimed.clues.sending

The Vancouver Art Gallery
///serious.food.bouncing

Simon Fraser University
///complain.puns.sprawls

Harbour Green Park

WEST HASTINGS STREET
WEST PENDER STREET

Browse the BILL REID GALLERY
One of the most well-known showcases of Indigenous art, the gallery has large-scale sculptures and a focus on Coast Salish artists. 5

DOWNTOWN

The **Vancouver Art Gallery** *always has Indigenous art in its exhibitions. Visit on a Tuesday for by-donation entry 5–8pm.*

0 meters 250
0 yards 250

CANADA PLACE

HORNBY STREET

DUNSMUIR STREET

RICHARDS STREET

CAMBIE STREET

ABBOTT STREET

WEST HASTINGS STREET

WEST PENDER STREET

WEST GEORGIA STREET

Experience
THE WINDS AND WATERS WILL ALWAYS CALL US HOME

Painted by Indigenous artist Ocean Hyland of Tsleil-Waututh Nation, this mural is a celebration of the interconnectedness of life and the importance of ocean sustainability.

6

Pop into
COASTAL PEOPLES FINE ARTS GALLERY

With many First Nations and Inuit-designed artworks for sale, this is a great spot for art aficionados and collectors. And if you're not in the market to buy? You're still welcome to look.

Wander through
SNÉKWEM LANE

This alley-long mural depicts a Squamish Nation story about how salmon came to the local waterways, guided by the sun (snékwem).

4

2

The Audain Gallery at **Simon Fraser University** *hosts art exhibitions, talks, and events inspired by contemporary Indigenous art.*

3

Stop by
CATHEDRAL SQUARE

This once-drab park is now home to the first collaborative art piece by artists from all First Nations whose territory Vancouver occupies.

1

Pay a visit to
SKWACHÀYS LODGE

Located in a hotel, this fair trade gallery offers visitors a chance to see the neighborhood through the eyes of urban Indigenous artists.

NIGHTLIFE

Whether it's a low-key evening of games in a retro arcade or a full-on night of dancing in a pulsating club, options for fun after dark are plentiful.

Live Music

High rents and licensing laws have hit Vancouver's music scene hard (the number of venue closures has even led to the nickname "No Fun City"), but these survivors prove it won't disappear without a fight.

THE HEATLEY

Map 5; 696 E Hastings Street, Strathcona; ///pink.examples.lately; www.heatley.ca

Possibly more than any other neighborhood, Strathcona is serious about its community-minded, working-class roots. And you can feel it when you enter The Heatley, a small bar with friendly staff and an "everyone is welcome" vibe. There are no pretentious musos here. Just down-to-earth folk ready to nod along to acoustic singer-songwriters and glory in the retro sounds of vinyl-loving DJs.

GUILT & CO

Map 2; 1 Alexander Street, Gastown; ///muddle.carrots.brains; www.guiltandcompany.com

Make sure you're in your dancing shoes; things can get pretty wild at this inviting underground space. Incredible local musicians and international guests take to the stage every night, drawing an

Guilt & Co has two music shows a night. The 7pm one is a great start to an evening out in Gastown.

eclectic mix of enthusiastic music lovers. More of a wallflower than a mover and shaker? No worries. Take a seat at one of the cozy tables and enjoy the show.

THE FOX CABARET

Map 4; 2321 Main Street, Mount Pleasant; ///invent.making.improves; www.foxcabaret.com

As a former porn theater, it's fair to say that The Fox has something of a colorful past. Not that you'd know it today. After a very thorough clean in 2014, the place has found a new lease of life as one of the city's top nightclubs. The locals have never looked back. Every week, faithful fans flock here for album-release events by local artists and pumping gigs from up-and-coming indie and hip-hop acts.

» **Don't leave without** popping upstairs for a nightcap at sibling venue The Projection Room, a tiny cocktail bar with live DJs.

THE COMMODORE BALLROOM

Map 1; 868 Granville Street, Downtown; ///classics.boot.blanked; www.commodoreballroom.com

The Clash, U2, Nirvana – name a band or artist, and chances are they've rocked the Commodore at some point. This restored 1920s ballroom is tailor-made for epic gigs. Amazing sound? Yep. Perfect sightlines? You got it. Sprung dance floor? Why, yes, now you mention it. A hangover from the venue's ballroom days, it gets the crowd bouncing and keeps the energy flowing throughout the entire space.

Solo, Pair, Crowd

No matter if it's just you and the music, or you and your friends, there's a venue ready and waiting.

FLYING SOLO
Keep it chill

Bacchus Lounge *(p67)*, in the Wedgewood Hotel & Spa, is the sort of place where tuxedoed servers pour your martini tableside. Raise a glass to the good life while enjoying soothing live piano music.

IN A PAIR
That's cool, man

The talent onstage at Frankie's Jazz Club is mostly local, but big names occasionally drop in for surprise sets. Bonus: the venue's menu of Italian classics is perfect for sharing with a friend.

FOR A CROWD
Rock out with your pals

You'd never guess Adele made her Vancouver debut in the 450-capacity Red Room. These days, metal and EDM are the favored genres, ideal for a wild (and loud) night on the dance floor with your crew.

2ND FLOOR GASTOWN

Map 2; 300 Water Street, Gastown; ///diner.blog.cuter;
www.waterstreetcafe.ca/2nd-floor-gastown

Upstairs from the Water St. Café, 2nd Floor Gastown manages to feel classy without being the least bit stuffy. There's no stage here; jazz bands and soloists merely set up in the corner and do their thing while couples cuddle up at candlelit tables.

CALABASH BISTRO

Map 2; 428 Carrall Street, Downtown Eastside;
///huddled.carry.surveyed; www.calabashbistro.com

This glorious combination of restaurant, bar, and venue keeps Caribbean music fans returning again and again. Midweek, they huddle around the stage listening to intimate sets by small bands and solo acts; come the weekend, they energetically unwind on the dance floor to the beat of live DJs.

THE LOBBY LOUNGE

Map 1; 1038 Canada Place, Coal Harbour; ///accusing.types.stays;
www.lobbyloungerawbar.com

Sweaty crowds and deafening volumes not your thing? Head to The Lobby Lounge, where you'll find a far more civilized scene. Settle into a comfy chair, order a cocktail, and enjoy the strains of a local jazz trio or classical pianist.

» Don't leave without wandering across the street to Coal Harbour and soaking up breathtaking views of the North Shore mountains.

LGBTQ2S+ Scene

The heart and soul of Vancouver's LGBTQ2S+ scene is Davie Village, located (surprise, surprise) along Davie Street. Here, the city's most inclusive lounge bars and clubs promise a truly fabulous night out.

1181 LOUNGE

Map 1; 1181 Davie Street, West End; ///plot.stretch.crunchy; www.eleven-81.com

It might be one of the smallest venues along the Davie Street strip, but 1181 Lounge sure packs a large punch. Think shirtless bartenders, colorful LED lights, and cocktails that take the edge off a hard week. It properly gets going around 11pm, when the Village's fun-loving fashionistas descend on the tiny-but-mighty dance floor to show off their moves.

CELEBRITIES NIGHTCLUB

Map 1; 1022 Davie Street, West End; ///audibly.mess.apples; www.celebritiesnightclub.com

Want an epic club night? Look no further than Celebrities, the biggest, most extravagant venue on the entire Davie circuit. World-famous DJs spin the decks on the stage, as ravers of all

Most evenings at Celebrities are ticketed, so check online and purchase yours in advance.

persuasions go wild in a dance frenzy. Expect to come out of here dripping in sweat, with a huge, happy smile on your face.

PUMPJACK PUB

Map 1; 1167 Davie Street, West End; ///admiral.curiosity.breathed; www.pumpjackpub.com

Crack the whip, and put your leather on – if that's what you're into, of course. Known as the "kink" spot in town, this pub draws a crowd of leather, daddy, and furry friends, and everything in between. Part pub, part nightclub, and even part billiards room, it's an inclusive space where you're free to pick your pleasure.

THE SCORE ON DAVIE

Map 1; 1262 Davie Street, West End; ///kings.blast.schools; https://scoreondavie.com

Come game day, this spot is packed with a welcoming bunch of sports fans, eyes glued to the many flat screens that surround the bar. While there's no guarantee that your team will actually, you know, score (we're looking at you, Canucks), the atmosphere here is always warm-hearted, with patrons bonded by a shared love of sports, beers, and epic pub grub.

» Don't leave without having your drink and eating it, too. The Score is famed for its Caesar cocktails, which come topped with everything from onion rings to chicken wings, and even burgers.

THE FOUNTAINHEAD PUB

**Map 1; 1025 Davie Street, West End; ///fixture.truck.routine;
https://thefountainheadpub.com**

Looking for something a bit more chilled? The Fountainhead is
the ideal spot to while away an afternoon around a pool table,
sipping local beer, and snacking on classic comfort food. And
who knows, when the evening revelers arrive for their first stop
on the Davie party circuit, you might just be tempted to continue
with them to the next one.

THE JUNCTION

**Map 1; 1138 Davie Street, West End; ///curtains.returns.sporting;
www.junctionpub.com**

Pinning The Junction down under one banner is tricky — and
that's exactly why it's so special. This rainbow-flag-flying bar,
club, restaurant, and events venue is the heart and soul of the

One of the oldest gay
institutions in the city, the
Bayside Lounge *(www.bayside
lounge.ca)*, at the very end
of Davie Street, is a secret
favorite of the local LGBTQ2S+
community. Tucked away from
the mainstream bars and
clubs at the heart of Davie
Village, it will take you back in
time with its retro 70s design
and large circular central bar.
Order a cocktail and enjoy the
sunset over English Bay.

Davie Village social scene. Locals can be found here every day of the week, getting competitive over bingo, laughing uproariously at a riotous drag performance, or tearing up the dance floor to the beats of a well-known DJ.

MARY'S ON DAVIE

Map 1; 1202 Davie Street, West End; ///symphony.bells.unveils; https://marysondavie.com

With its stylish retro design and vibrant green-and-pink pastel color palette, this cheery diner couldn't be more social media-friendly if it tried. (It doesn't hurt that it's right next to the Village's photogenic rainbow crosswalk, either). Join local influencers grabbing a cheeky cocktail and a bite to eat after snapping perfectly curated pics for their feed.

NUMBERS CABARET

Map 1; 1042 Davie Street, West End; ///radio.fork.nuance; https://numbers.ca

In the mood to dance? There's only one place to go: Numbers. This narrow venue knows how to party, with colorful rainbow lights and multiple rooms filled with carefree revelers busting a move. It's loud and it's sweaty, and it's exactly how the locals like it. Just take a look at the line outside for proof: it stretches all the way down the block every Friday and Saturday night.

» **Don't leave without** making a plan to come back and show off your vocals in the Karaoke Room on Sunday.

Cool Clubs

Walk through the neon-lit entertainment district of Granville Street and you'll find a city that likes to party. Stay there for clubs with swank and style, or venture further afield into the city's edgy underground scene.

LEVELS NIGHTCLUB

Map 1; 560 Seymour Street, Downtown; ///themes.reaction.lifts; https://levelsvancouver.ca

Of all Vancouver's nightclubs, you can count on Levels to live up to your epic EDM expectations. A dance floor that spans three stories? Check. International artists bumping beats through a massive sound system? Check. Every laser and light known to ravekind? Check and check. With bottle service to get the party started, you'll be reluctant to leave the glow sticks behind at closing time.

TWELVE WEST

Map 1; 1219 Granville Street, Downtown; ///nutrients.happier.usages; https://twelvewest.ca

Twelve West is where the local VIP set go when they're in the mood for a proper night out. True, it's pricey and not easy to get in, but you get what you pay for: dance floor-filling mainstream beats,

Table service can be transferred between Twelve West and sister club The Mansion – just ask the host.

sparkling bottle service, and opulent decor that will make you feel expensive just by being there. Get your name on the guest list and come dressed to impress.

FORTUNE SOUND CLUB

Map 2; 147 E Pender Street, Chinatown; ///animate.motivations.trace; www.fortunesoundclub.com

Looking for an off-the-beaten-path club with more grit and grime than the Granville strip? Fortune it is. At this sweaty dance fest, electronic and hip-hop DJs are revered like royalty by the unpretentious crowd. The music is loud, the moves are wild, and the energy is utterly infectious.

>> Don't leave without stopping by neighboring Pizza Coming Soon for a pre-drink bite. Just don't expect to get any pizza – it's actually a funky Japanese snack bar.

PARADISE

Map 2; 238 Keefer Street, Chinatown; ///required.tweeted.shuffle; https://paradiseyvr.com

Keep your eyes peeled for the underground entrance to Paradise, an unassuming basement venue where house and techno fans gather for after-hours raves. Inside, the decor is as minimal as the signage out front; all the attention has instead been lavished on the truly spectacular sound system. It's one of the city's best-kept rave secrets – but you didn't hear it from us.

Liked by the locals

"People are bored of the same old club scene, but when you come to Gallery, you get all of the elements of a Vegas-style nightclub. It doesn't exist anywhere in Canada, so it's something completely new."

ANDONIS POMONIS, GALLERY VANCOUVER'S
PRESIDENT OF OPERATIONS

THE BASEMENT & THE LIVING ROOM

Map 1; 654 Nelson Street, Downtown; ///hilltop.parkway.smaller;
www.hotelbelmont.ca/eat-and-drink

Tucked below the Belmont Hotel, this fun-loving, not-quite-a-club
is like an elevated house party thrown by cool kids whose parents
are away. Make like you're one of the popular crowd and grab a
cocktail at the main lounge (aka Living Room), before heading down
to The Basement to let loose on the dance floor.

» Don't leave without throwing a strike at the five-pin bowling alley,
one of many nostalgic surprises found in The Basement.

OMBRE SHOW LOUNGE

Map 2; 350 Water Street, Gastown; ///launch.intent.thinking;
www.ombreshowlounge.com

Wannabe B-boys (and some real ones) come to bust a move at this
hip-hop club. Crammed tight with young folks and running regular
theme nights (including Y2K and Destiny's Child throwbacks), it's the
perfect place to show off your street dancing skills.

GALLERY

Map 6; 1312 SW Marine Drive, Marpole; ///hobbit.donation.silence;
https://galleryvancouver.com

Fancy a night out Vegas-style? You better head to Gallery. Inside,
revelers are greeted by a riot of exotic dancers, indoor fireworks, and
acrobats swinging from the ceiling. Oh, and there's a dance floor
somewhere in there, too. So much for Vancouver being "No Fun City."

Comedy Shows

Vancouver may not have an international reputation for comedy, but it's not down to lack of talent – there's actually an incredible stand-up scene. Here are the shows that locals can't get enough of.

JOKES PLEASE!

Map 4; 326 W 5th Avenue, Mount Pleasant; ///restore.snoring.possibly; www.eventbrite.ca/o/jokes-please-31441829869

Looking for a fun start to the weekend? Join the merry Friday-night crowd for Jokes Please! at The Cambrian Hall. One of Vancouver's longest-running comedy shows, it's where you'll find your favorite stand-ups from Netflix, HBO, and Just for Laughs. Tickets go quickly, but don't despair if they're sold out; there's a second show on Saturdays at The RCC in Kitsilano.

TIGHTROPE THEATRE

Map 4; 2343 Main Street, Mount Pleasant; ///stubborn.skip.graphics; https://tightropetheatre.com

Shows by the energetic improv team at Tightrope provoke more than just belly laughs – they'll have you giggling, screaming, and crying, sometimes all at the same time. Input from the ever-enthusiastic audience is actively encouraged, with particularly raucous results at the late-night "Dirty Little Secrets" show (held monthly on Fridays), where guests anonymously submit secrets for the troupe to explore on stage. Share if you dare.

COMEDY AFTER DARK

Map 2; 117 W Pender Street, Downtown; ///fuzzy.payback.indirect; https://comedyafterdark.ca

True to its name, Comedy After Dark is uncensored and definitely not for kids. Embrace the vibe by ordering a stiff drink, then settle back to enjoy the latest lineup of amateur and professional comedians, who get the crowd roaring with laughter (and occasionally horror) at some of the things that come out of their mouths.

» Don't leave without indulging in the epic happy hour menu, available 6–7pm and 9pm–close every Sunday–Thursday. Who can resist a $6 Jameson Pickle Back?

THE SUNDAY SERVICE

Map 4; 2321 Main Street, Mount Pleasant; ///myth.blending.cost; www.thesundayservice.ca

Sundays are sacred in Vancouver – but not in the way you might think. After filling up on baked eggs and French toast during the ritual morning brunch, faithful comedy fans round off the day by congregating at the Fox Cabaret (p137) to watch The Sunday Service Improv Company. Always hilarious, this eclectic group of goof-arounds convert a new group of disciples every time.

THE COMEDY RING

Map 2; 433 W Pender Street, Gastown; ///flight.blizzard.soldiers; https://comedyring.carrd.co

With regular shows at Holy Chow restaurant, plus so many other spaces in the city, there are plenty of opportunities to catch the reliably funny Comedy Ring troupe. But be warned: the comics are known to pick on the audience, so make sure to come with some thick skin.

THE IMPROV CENTRE

Map 3; 1502 Duranleau Street, Granville Island; ///rungs.detection.relaxing; https://theimprovcentre.ca

Silliness abounds at the Improv Centre, a veritable Vancouver institution. As good-humored as their down-to-earth audience, the theater's ensemble of over 40 performers are famed for uproarious improvisational shows that are never the same twice. (And genuinely, some people go back multiple times.) Popular weekly events include Theatresports, where two teams compete for the biggest laughs,

Try it!
AN INTRO TO IMPROV

Feeling brave? The Improv Centre offers two-hour drop-in workshops every Saturday, where you can cast aside your inhibitions and learn the basics of improv with a group of new friends.

while unforgettable temporary productions have included the
Agatha Christie-inspired "Stage Fright: Murder at the Improv."
The space itself is simple and small, so when that lady in the front
row starts snorting uncontrollably, you can't help but join in.

» **Don't leave without** reliving the funniest bits over a post-show
drink in the theater's welcoming bar.

CHILL PILL COMEDY
Map 3; 1184 Denman Street, West End; ///unusually.dividing.scarves; www.eventbrite.ca/o/chill-pill-comedy-34149685093

In true casual Vancouver style, Chill Pill is one of the most relaxed
comedy nights around. Held every Thursday at the Loft Lounge, a
bright and airy Caribbean restaurant in the West End, it's perfect
for a laid-back night out with friends. Arrive early to catch up over
dinner and cocktails, then spin your seat to face the stage for an
eye-wateringly funny stand-up set.

MOON BASED COMEDY
Map 5; 1212 Commercial Drive, East Van; ///posed.revisit.unless; www.havanavancouver.com

Featuring up-and-coming local comedians, and hosted by partners
Robyn Pekar and Jackie Hoffart, Moon Based Comedy celebrates
everything feminist, queer, and diverse in the world of funny folk.
Twice-monthly shows are held in the Eastside's Havana Theatre,
with a separate one in The Projection Room (at The Fox Cabaret,
see p137) – and, occasionally, the odd bonus event in a local backyard.

Games Night

A night out in Vancouver doesn't necessarily mean all-out partying – the laid-back locals are just as happy having a low-key evening playing retro arcade games, ping-pong, or pool.

GLITCH

Map 3; 2287 W Broadway, Kitsilano; ///flasks.twin.cover; www.glitchvancouver.com

This retro arcade bar is seriously lit, and not just because of the glow that emanates from the bar and the pinball and skeeball machines. No, it's a 4,000-sq-ft (372-sq-m) manifestation of what every '80s and '90s video game-loving kid wished their room looked like. Hit up your bestie and live out your childhood fantasies while sipping on boozy slushies.

GRETA BAR YVR

Map 2; 50 W Cordova Street, Gastown; ///fizzy.cleans.alive; www.gretabar.com

Casual nights out don't get much cooler than this souped-up adults-only arcade bar. Exposed brick walls, colorful murals, and food-truck inspired eats create a trendy hipster vibe, while games like Guitar Hero and air hockey lure competitive groups of pals from all over town. Even better: there's also a dance floor for those who want to let loose without hitting the clubs.

» **Don't leave without** trading in your tickets from your night's winnings for some swag, like beanies and T-shirts branded with the Greta Bar logo.

THE AMERICAN

Map 2; 926 Main Street , Strathcona; ///zealous.drums.credited; https://theamerican.bar

Few things get Vancouverites more riled up than a Canucks game, when the city's ardent hockey fans come together to yell at the big screen. And one place you can be sure to find them is The American. Part arcade and part sports bar, this relaxed venue not only screens the most important NHL games, but also caters to all sorts of NFL, NBA, and other sports fans. If the tension starts to get a bit much (or the Canucks are on yet another losing streak), the pool table and pinball machines offer the perfect distraction.

Try it!
GO FOR GLORY

Consider yourself a pinball wizard? Test your prowess by entering The American's weekly Wednesday-night tournament. There's also bingo straight after if you want to go for the double.

Solo, Pair, Crowd

Vancouver has plenty of places where you and your friends can show off your trivia knowledge.

FLYING SOLO

Join a Taphouse team

Struggling to get a team together? Wednesday nights at the casual Malone's Taphouse, in the heart of Downtown, are perfect for meeting fellow trivia lovers who'll welcome you into the fold.

IN A PAIR

Feeling lucky

Next date night, forget about the usual romantic dinner for two. Instead book a table for the Thursday trivia night at BC Kitchen in the Parq Casino; you can hit the gaming tables after, if you fancy.

FOR A CROWD

It's game time

Gather the gang and make a night of it, starting with Tuesday trivia at Relish Pub. Afterward, stay out until the early hours gorging on late-night bites and seeking out live music on the Granville Strip.

BACK AND FORTH BAR

Map 2; 303 Columbia Street, Gastown; ///skill.connects.debit;
www.backandforthbar.com

Whether you're a pro or a newbie, you're welcome at the ping-pong tables in this down-to-earth dive bar. Competition is fierce but friendly, with the constant clack of balls and paddles providing a steady soundtrack for the waiting players sat around the bar.
» Don't leave without sampling the long lineup of cheap and local craft beers, from the likes of Twin Sails, Parallel 49, and Phillips.

SOHO BAR & BILLIARDS

Map 1; 1283 Hamilton Street, Yaletown; ///ending.treaties.terms;
www.sohobar.ca

With all its bougie, yuppie-filled bars, Yaletown doesn't seem like the obvious choice for a no-frills night out. But, as local residents will tell you, there are still some casual spots if you know where to look. The top pick is Soho Bar & Billiards, with pool tables, foosball, pinball, and darts, plus a menu of classic drinks that won't break the bank.

THE DEN

Map 3; 1348 Robson Street, West End; ///whom.peachy.frantic;
www.thedenvancouver.com

Tough day? Forget your troubles at this chill, basement-like hangout. As you lose yourself in games like Pacman and skeeball, the '80s tunes from the jukebox provide a hit of feel-good nostalgia. There's no kitchen, but patrons can bring their own food. Hickory Sticks it is then.

An evening out in
Gastown

Originally a rough settlement for the logging trade, Gastown is one of Vancouver's oldest quarters. In fact, it was Canada's third-largest city until it became part of Vancouver in 1886 – though it was hardly its pride and joy. Seedy and run down, the area was often described as a stereotypical "skid row" (the term comes from the practice of skidding timber down the street) and a strict ban on alcohol was put in place for workers at the lumber mill. While it retains some of its grit, Gastown is now a hub of bustling restaurants and lively bars where the booze flows freely.

1. Pourhouse
162 Water Street; www.
pourhousevancouver.com
///earlobe.rugs.finds

2. Monarca
181 Carrall Street; www.
monarcavancouver.ca
///returns.expose.moved

3. Guilt & Co
1 Alexander Street; www.
guiltandcompany.com
///muddle.carrots.brains

4. The Diamond
6 Powell Street;
www.di6mond.com
///dragon.underway.secures

5. Gringo
27 Blood Alley Square;
www.gringorestaurants.com
///visions.rings.leads

📍 **Blood Alley**
///abode.normal.surround

WEST WATERFRONT ROAD

GASTOWN

WATER STREET

1

**Sip a cocktail at
POURHOUSE**
No one takes cocktails more seriously than this Vancouver institution. Start your evening with a drink at this century-old warehouse conversion.

CAMBIE ST

WEST PENDER ST

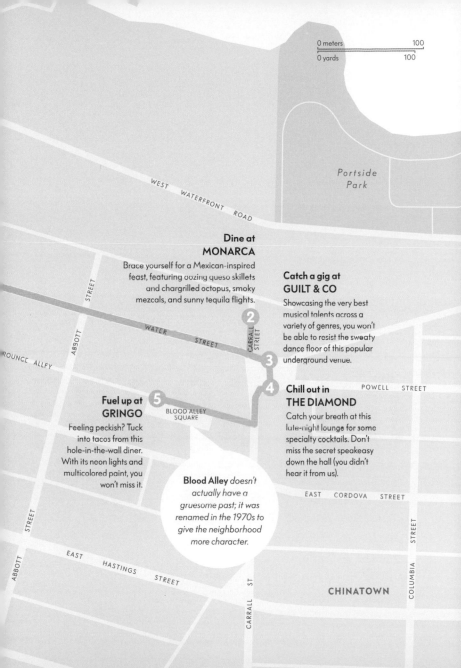

Portside Park

WEST WATERFRONT ROAD

Dine at
MONARCA

Brace yourself for a Mexican-inspired feast, featuring oozing queso skillets and chargrilled octopus, smoky mezcals, and sunny tequila flights.

Catch a gig at
GUILT & CO

Showcasing the very best musical talents across a variety of genres, you won't be able to resist the sweaty dance floor of this popular underground venue.

STREET

ABBOTT

ROUNCE ALLEY

WATER STREET

CARRALL STREET

2

3

4

POWELL STREET

Fuel up at
GRINGO

Feeling peckish? Tuck into tacos from this hole-in-the-wall diner. With its neon lights and multicolored paint, you won't miss it.

5

BLOOD ALLEY SQUARE

Chill out in
THE DIAMOND

Catch your breath at this late-night lounge for some specialty cocktails. Don't miss the secret speakeasy down the hall (you didn't hear it from us).

Blood Alley *doesn't actually have a gruesome past; it was renamed in the 1970s to give the neighborhood more character.*

EAST CORDOVA STREET

STREET

ABBOTT

STREET

EAST HASTINGS STREET

CARRALL ST

COLUMBIA STREET

CHINATOWN

OUTDOORS

With the city's blissful Pacific coastline and lush medley of peaks, parks, and rainforests, it's no wonder locals live and breathe the natural world.

Green Spaces

Vancouver's trails and leafy parks are where locals start or end the work day. Whether it's a morning jog, a lunchtime picnic, or an after-dinner stroll among the cedars, the city's parks have you covered.

WHYTE LAKE

Map 6; Trans Canada Highway, West Vancouver;
///marginal.trailing.guarded

Seeking plans for a weekend outdoors? Make like a local and set your alarm for an early morning hike in West Vancouver's hills. The tranquil surroundings of towering fir trees and trickling creeks provide a soothing start to the day. At the end of the trail is a small lake where you can invigorate yourself with a refreshing dip – or a friendly game of ice hockey, depending on the season.

STANLEY PARK

Map 3; Start at 1929 W Georgia Street, Downtown;
///spilling.mere.audible; https://vancouver.ca

As integral to Vancouver as Central Park is to New York City, this 1,000-acre (400 ha) oasis is the city's wild centerpiece. Stanley Park runs in the blood of every local, the green backdrop to countless perfect memories. This is where children learn to cycle on the scenic seawall, friends tan on the sandy beaches, and enviably sprightly retirees stroll the forested trails. A city as nature-loving as Vancouver deserves an iconic park – thankfully, it has Stanley.

» Don't leave without seeking out the park's collection of totem poles to learn the stories of the area's First Nations.

PACIFIC SPIRIT REGIONAL PARK

Map 6; 4915 W 16th Avenue, UBC; ///admires.keep.smooth;
www.metrovancouver.org

After a stressful week in class, UBC students have one place on their minds: Pacific Spirit Regional Park. There are no bad grades or deadlines here, just mile after mile of sprawling trails, clean air, and lush rainforest canopy. Bring your hiking boots or bike, and enjoy some well-deserved time out.

There are two ways to the top of Grouse Mountain, which is fondly nicknamed the "Peak of Vancouver." There's the uber-popular Grouse Grind, a grueling 1.5-mile (2.5km) trail, comprising 2,830 steps. Or try the BCMC trail, slightly longer but mercifully less steep and less busy. In the evenings, keep your eyes peeled for the owls which nestle in the mountain's treetops. And whichever route you take, here's a tip: take the Skyride gondola back down.

CAPILANO RIVER REGIONAL PARK

Map 6; 5077 Dam Road, North Vancouver; ///repeated.expired.contacts;
www.metrovancouver.org

A word of advice: be careful not to confuse this with the super-touristy Capilano Suspension Bridge Park just down the road. There, you'll find tour groups and admission fees. Here, you'll instead have lush, green paths and free picnic spots all to yourself (except for the occasional trail runner or two). The park's even got its own rival bridges. Okay, they're not quite as fun as the suspension bridge, but the views over the Capilano River canyon are just as dramatic.

LYNN CANYON

Map 6; 3690 Park Road, North Vancouver; ///kickers.props.stacks;
https://lynncanyon.ca

Nothing showcases Vancouver's charming ecosystem of green spaces better than the trails of Lynn Canyon. From this verdant retreat, forest-clad paths connect the region's other green lungs, including Lynn Headwaters and Rice Lake. These routes seem

Try it!
GET A GUIDE

Feel daunted by solo hiking? Why not join a group trip or hire a guide to take you out. BeWild Adventures (*www.bewildadventures. com*) offers numerous options, from waterfall walks to full-day rambles.

designed to convince you that you've left the city entirely, as they bypass natural pools, glimmering lakes, and swaying canyon bridges. Best of all, the paths remain quiet even at the height of summer, a perfect reason to take the road less traveled.

LIGHTHOUSE PARK

Map 6; 4902 Beacon Lane, West Vancouver;
///immunity.healers.displays; https://westvancouver.ca

Spring afternoons are just made for ambling around Lighthouse Park. Not only has it got a bucketload of scenery (like Western red cedars, Douglas firs, and sparkling views of the Pacific), but the trails are gentle enough that you'll barely break a sweat. The rocky outcrops along the coast make for an idyllic place to picnic while gazing at the park's namesake lighthouse. Keep your eyes peeled for wildlife while you're at it – if you're lucky, you might see a bald eagle.

» Don't leave without venturing to Juniper Point to watch the sunset – it's a low-stakes hike for a high reward.

INTER RIVER PARK

Map 6; 2000 Lillooet Road, North Vancouver; ///copper.runners.boomed

This multi-use park is popular with everyone from hardy BMXers to sauntering dog walkers. But the reason we love it? It's a great place to combine a hike with a wild swim. Simply head north and follow the Baden-Powell Trail, looking out for pathways to the creek on the left. It's dotted with inviting swimming holes, which buzz on sunny weekends with lively groups of friends enjoying a refreshing (read: chilly) dip.

Scenic Cycles

Biking in Vancouver isn't just a way to get around, it's a way of life. The city's passion for cycling is reflected in its weaving bike lanes, lush gravel trails, hip rental shops, and bike shares.

ARBUTUS GREENWAY

Map 3; Start at 6th Avenue at Fir Street, Kitsilano; ///siesta.slab.boat

You really can't go wrong with this super-safe and super-scenic bike trail, which acts as the city's main north–south thoroughfare for two-wheelers. Our tip? Start at the north end at 6th and Fir in Kitsilano. It just so happens to be the exact location of Beaucoup Bakery – basically a sign from the universe to pick up a flaky French pastry to fuel your pedal-powered adventure.

SPIRIT TRAIL

Map 6; Start at 759 E 3rd Street, North Shore; ///object.gateway.offline

Vancouver has lots of pretty shoreline trails, and this is one of our favorites. Built by local North Shore municipalities and the Squamish First Nation, this 4-mile (6.5-km) paved pathway will eventually connect Deep Cove to the ferry terminal at Horseshoe Bay. For now, start your day at Moodyville Park and cycle toward

Keep your eye out for local birdlife, especially at Moodyville Park, a popular spot for nesting bald eagles.

the Shipyards and Lonsdale Quay, where you can stop for a coffee at the market, visit the Polygon Gallery, or have a beer at House of Funk brewing.

STANLEY PARK SEAWALL

Map 3; Start at W Georgia Street and Denman Street, Coal Harbour; ///eyelid.sounds.thrones

The seawall is truly the crown jewel of Vancouver's cycle routes, as loved by casual commuters as it is by spandex-clad bike bros. Pick up a Mobi cycle share or rental in Coal Harbour (grab a tandem if you're looking for a laugh), then pedal your way past the Brockton Point lighthouse toward the iconic Siwash Rock and Third Beach. Your attention will inevitably be fixed on the glittering Pacific, but do keep to the ocean-hugging cycle lane, as the route can get packed.

» Don't leave without riding the seawall out of Stanley Park and over the Art Deco-style Burrard Street Bridge, which has a safe bike lane and amazing aerial views of False Creek and English Bay.

FISHERMAN'S TRAIL

Map 6; Start at the end of Lillooet Road, North Shore; ///blur.basher.little

Never fancied off-road biking? Give the Fisherman's Trail a go and you might just be convinced otherwise. The well-maintained route along the pristine Seymour River offers gentle hills, fresh forest air, and views over shimmering mountain ranges to the east. A round trip is 7 miles (12 km), a perfect intro to the joys of the gravel trail.

Liked by the locals

"There's something special about riding westbound along the Adanac bike path at sunset. With so few cars in the way, I glide toward the colorfully lit city and feel gratitude to live where I do."

DANIELA GUNN-DOERGE,
AVID CYCLIST AND DAILY BIKE COMMUTER

ADANAC BIKE PATH

Map 5; Start at Main Street and Union Street, Strathcona;
///cuts.intend.wardrobe

The go-to commuter path connecting East Van to Downtown, the Adanac ("Canada," spelled backward) is like the Autobahn for cyclists. Here, come rain or shine, locals bike to and from work at warp speed. The path might not be the city's most tranquil, but racing through Vancouver's residential heartlands will make you feel local in no time. If you want to really look the part, head east on the Union-Adanac corridor and stop by the Landyachtz bike shop to scope its drool-worthy custom frames.

VANCOUVER TO STEVESTON

Map 4; Start at W 2nd Avenue and Ontario Street, Mount Pleasant;
///removed.square.talents

If you want to better understand the local obsession with cycling, hit up the West Dyke Trail on a summer evening. Heading toward the pretty fishing village of Steveston, in the distance you'll have postcard-perfect views over the Fraser River. Closer at hand, young couples and families coast leisurely along the safe, flat, and well-maintained cycle path. Great times with loved ones in the great outdoors – this is exactly what cycling means to the city. The route takes most riders under two hours to finish, and if you toast your arrival in Steveston with a deserved sundowner, you can always take the bike-friendly Canada Line SkyTrain back.

» Don't leave without noshing on some fish and chips at Pajo's or Dave's, or buying seafood from the Fisherman's Wharf to cook at home.

On the Water

*It would be criminal to live right next to all these
lakes and the Pacific, only to simply stare at them.
Luckily, ever-active Vancouverites have come up with
tons of ways to go adventuring out on the water.*

SUP AT KITS BEACH

**Map 3; Vancouver Water Adventures, 1812 Boatlift Lane, Kitsilano;
///jumped.digs.coiling; www.vancouverwateradventures.com**

If you can take a sport and make it even more intense, you better
believe Vancouverites will do it – they've even turned leisurely
stand-up paddleboarding into a high-speed racing league. But
there's no rule that says you have to go quite that hard. Instead, rent
an SUP from Vancouver Water Adventures at Kits Beach and
meander the coastline, feeling zen.

CANOEING AT PITT LAKE

**Map 6; Pitt Lake 4 Canoe Rental, 19090 Rannie Road, Pitt Meadows;
///landings.roaming.stilts; https://pitt-lake-canoe-rental.business.site**

Paddling Pitt Lake might make for a beautiful day trip, but beware:
the area is known for its Sasquatch (Bigfoot) sightings. Grab a boat
from Pitt Lake 4 Canoe Rental and paddle over to Pinecone Burke

Pitt Lake is tidal, so make sure you pull your boat well out of the water when you take a break.

Provincial Park, where you can hike up to Widgeon Falls. Or, if you don't mind roughing it, camp for the night. Just keep an eye out for ape-sized footprints.

WHALE WATCHING

Map 3; Prince of Whales, 1666 Duranleau Street, Granville Island; ///delight.worth.crunchy; https://princeofwhales.com

Spotting a whale top of your bucket list? You're in the right city. Though many whale species migrate through Vancouver waterways, orcas are undoubtedly the main attraction. And from March to October, there's a good chance of seeing J-Pod, the beloved local killer whale squad, on a tour with local company Prince of Whales. The rest of the year? Take a sea safari through Howe Sound instead.

KAYAKING IN DEEP COVE

Map 6 Deep Cove Kayak, 2156 Banbury Road, North Vancouver; ///scramble.resolved.prelude; www.deepcovekayak.com

To experience deep calm in Deep Cove, pick up a boat from Deep Cove Kayaks, dip your paddle into the slow waters, and float off. Before long, you'll come face-to-face with curious seals, gliding lazily alongside you. Paddle over to Twin Islands for a picnic, where you can admire the fjord (as the seals admire your lunch). Just make sure you leave no trace: you're on the seals' turf now.

» **Don't leave without** trying a donut from Honey's café nearby — they're Kate Winslet's favorites (apparently), and will be yours, too.

Solo, Pair, Crowd

Whether you're a lone sailor or cruising with a crew, Vancouver's got what you need to get out on the water.

FLYING SOLO

I'm on a boat

Join the line of Downtown commuters and Granville Island tourists and hop on an Aquabus, the city's super-fun little water taxis. It's a great way to zip between docks scattered along the shores of False Creek.

IN A PAIR

Sunset cruise for two

It's a little cheesy, but a dinner cruise is a fun way to watch the sun set over the harbor with your other half. Many tours turn into a late-night party, so the two of you can dance under the stars.

FOR A CROWD

Floating BBQ with the crew

Like a view with your dinner? Take things a step further with Joe's BBQ Boats. Your party of eight can pile into an inflatable vessel and putter around False Creek while grilling your own gourmet meal.

KITE- AND WINDSURFING IN SQUAMISH

Map 6; Squamish Watersports, 38124 Loggers Lane, Squamish;
///storage.think.enormous; www.squamishwatersports.com

Forget caffeine. In Vancouver, weekends begin with a shot of extreme sport adrenaline. If that sounds like your cup of intensity, drive up the Sea to Sky inlet to Squamish, B.C.'s kite- and windsurfing haven. Ambitious beginners can take a lesson with Squamish Watersports; expect to swallow your pride and a big dose of saltwater.

FISHING CHARTER

Map 3; Bites On, Stamps Landing, False Creek; ///fame.snap.musician;
https://bites-on.com

The seals know it, the birds know it, the orcas know it: this region is off the hook for fishing. The knowledgeable local guides at Bites On Fishing Charters are more than happy to share their wisdom to help you catch your own salmon, Dungeness crab, or spot prawn dinner.

KAYAKING ON FALSE CREEK

Map 4; Creekside Kayaks, 1 Athletes Way, False Creek;
///darling.siesta.sitting; https://dragonzone.ca

Ironically, one of the best ways to see the city is not to be "in" the city at all, but rather in a kayak on the water. Stop by Creekside Kayaks and launch your boat at False Creek, soaking up the scenic skyline from the city's safest and most protected place to paddle.

» Don't leave without watching the impressively fast dragon boat teams training in the creek.

Beautiful Beaches

Whether it's for a morning stroll or a brisk plunge in the Pacific, the beach brings locals together no matter the weather. One thing's for sure: the ocean provides far more than Vancouver's dreamy backdrop.

KITS BEACH

Map 3; Cornwall Avenue at Yew Street, Kitsilano; ///cried.stick.somebody

Picture this. Bronzed volleyball players kick up sand as they serve a winning play. Beachgoers laze on towels around them, wandering to the water for a cheeky swim before retreating beneath the massive weeping willow trees for a shaded picnic or barbecue. Sound like summer paradise? That's because it is, which is why "Kits" is one of Vancouver's most popular beaches.

AMBLESIDE

Map 6; Marine Drive at 13th Street, West Vancouver; ///engages.bangle.hushed

The neighborhood of Ambleside is West Vancouver's artistic hub, and the ocean is the area's lifeblood. Home to the North Shore's largest sandy beach, in summer it has all the trappings of a perfect ocean vacation. Locals lounging on towels with the latest page

Parking can be scarce; look for a spot behind the Park Royal Centre Mall and take the trail to the beach.

turner? Check. Delicious food stands and picnic tables? Check. Playgrounds for the kids? Check. The area is bustling, and with good reason.

JERICHO AND SPANISH BANKS

Map 6; NW Marine Drive at Belmont Avenue, West Point Grey; ///creeps.belong.assures

On the southern shore of English Bay lie Jericho and Spanish Banks beaches. From their sandy expanse, you can take in stupefying views over Downtown to West Vancouver and beyond. This is the spot to marvel at the magic of a Pacific sunset, lighting up the mountainous horizon in flaming shades of red. With bonus points for being less trafficked than Kits, these spots are well worth the trip.
» Don't leave without seeing Jericho at low tide, when the beach extends so far you'll feel like you're walking into the center of the ocean.

WRECK BEACH

Map 6; 6572 NW Marine Drive, UBC; ///somebody.squad.client

Wreck Beach might offer some of the lushest west-facing views in the area, but most people aren't really here for the scenery. This clothing-optional beach is where locals come to hang loose, soaking up the beach's legendary peace-and-love vibes. So when city living becomes too much, shed those stresses (and clothes, if that's your thing) and make for Wreck. Just don't be alarmed when nude vendors come by to sell you boozy drinks – it's all part of the schtick.

CATES PARK

Map 6; 4141 Dollarton Highway, North Vancouver;
///repeats.similar.elbowed

Cates is also known by its ancestral name Whey-ah-Wichen – a Tsleil-Waututh First Nation word for "faces the wind." And for good reason. It's found at the end of the Indian Arm channel, which gets notoriously gusty in the afternoons. Visit in the morning when the breeze is milder, and look for the stairs down to the hidden (and protected) beach on the eastern side of the point. You'll usually have the tiny sandy shore to yourself, a perfect spot for a dip.

THIRD BEACH

Map 3; Stanley Park Drive at Tatlow Walk, Stanley Park;
///called.songs.science

After finishing up their workdays, young Vancouverites hop on their bikes to Third Beach – the go-to spot for an evening swim with friends. The beach is most spectacular on sunny Tuesday afternoons in summer, when the Brahm's Tams Drum Circle has gathered. This

Try it!
BEACHSIDE POOLS

If waves aren't your thing, take a seaside swim at one of the pools at Second Beach in Stanley Park or New Brighton in East Van. With heated water and sloped entries, you'll forget the icy Pacific.

renegade crew of percussionists slap on any available surface to make a beat while crowds sway to their rhythmic noise. It's a wild yet well-mannered affair that draws hundreds.

SUNSET BEACH AND ENGLISH BAY

Map 3; 1700 Beach Avenue, West End; ///hotspot.triads.shots

As Vancouver's long winter draws to a close, some things are certain: the maple trees will blossom, the mercury will rise, and locals will flock to Sunset Beach. Along with nearby English Bay, the beach is thronged in the hotter months with honeymooning couples, teens on Spring Break, and older folk topping up their Vitamin D. Take in the buzz from your towel, or people-watch from the Cactus Club patio at English Bay. There's no better place to thaw out.

» Don't leave without wandering over to the Inukshuk rock monument – a popular Inuit symbol traditionally used for navigation and marking important locations.

SANDY COVE BEACH

Map 6; 3966 Marine Drive, West Vancouver;
///fighters.manhole.exchanges

The best things in life are often the hardest to find. That certainly applies to Sandy Cove, which has no signposts and all but vanishes during high tide. Time your visit right, though, and you're in for a treat. Tucked between two rocky headlands, this petite cove strips beachgoing back to its basics: just heavenly golden sands, gently lapping waves, and the sun's warming caress. And, breathe.

Nearby Getaways

Vancouver might be magical, but with some of North America's most jaw-dropping mountains, coastlines, and lakes right on its doorstep, locals are often itching to hit the open road.

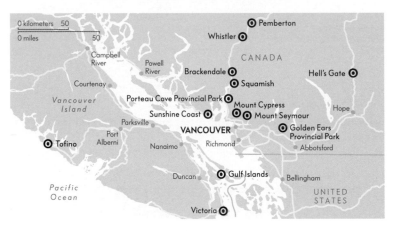

MOUNT CYPRESS

30-minute drive from the city; https://cypressmountain.com

At the first hint of snow, the city's slope lovers head straight to Mount Cypress. Here, crisp winter days are spent merrily cross-country skiing, tubing, and snowboarding — and warming up with the traditional après-ski, of course. Come summer, it's the hikers who are first to the mountain's alpine meadows, followed swiftly by the city's romantics. What's a mountain got to do with romance? It's the perfect place for a date night spent gazing at the stars.

PORTEAU COVE PROVINCIAL PARK

45-minute drive from the city; https://bcparks.ca

A word of warning: you'll need to book months in advance if you want to snag a spot at this wildly popular waterfront campsite. But don't worry if you miss out on a reservation. You're still welcome to swing by and spend a few delightful hours swimming serenely among octopi, sea anemones, and sunken boats, in the company of local scuba and free divers.

SQUAMISH

1-hour drive from the city; www.exploresquamish.com

This charming mountain town has exploded in popularity over the last decade, and it's no wonder why. Here, you're only a trail run away from the crème de la crème of British Columbia's wilderness. Why not spend a day bouldering on the granite bluffs overlooking Howe Sounds, whitewater rafting on the Cheakamus River, or snorkeling into Porteau Cove? If you have time for only one thing, we suggest a hike past the towering waterfalls in Shannon Falls Provincial Park. You can always round off a day well spent with a donut (or three) from the town's Sunflower Bakery & Cafe.

>> Don't leave without taking a boat tour – it's a fab way to see the area and the only way to access the beautifully secluded Echo Lake.

MOUNT SEYMOUR

30-minute drive from the city; https://mtseymour.ca

Only a 30-minute drive from Downtown, Mount Seymour is outdoor recreation central. Hiking, mountain biking, snowshoeing, skiing – you name it, Mount Seymour offers it. New to snow sports? You've come to the right place. The beginner-friendly bunny hill and relatively cheap lift pass make it a fantastic spot to find your feet (or should that be skis?).

WHISTLER

2-hour drive from the city; www.whistler.com

Among outdoor types, Whistler needs no introduction. This wild mountain playground offers ideal alpine terrain for all sorts of gnarly pursuits. Here in winter? Check out the world-class skiing and snowboarding at Whistler Blackcomb. How about summer? Join adrenaline junkies flying above the treetops on North America's longest zipline. And whatever the season, it never hurts to soak in the baths among the trees at the heavenly Scandinave Spa.

» Don't leave without posing for a photo in front of the iconic Olympic rings in Whistler Village.

BRACKENDALE

1-hour drive from the city; www.exploresquamish.com

Fun fact: this community at the northern end of Squamish is home to North America's largest population of wintering bald eagles. They're actually so important to the area that the Brackendale

Eagles Provincial Park has been set up specially for their protection. It's here you'll find twitchers from late October to early January, quietly huddled in the Eagle Run viewing shelter hoping to glimpse the majestic birds.

SUNSHINE COAST

2-hour drive from the city, including ferry ride to Gibsons;
www.sunshinecoastcanada.com

The relaxed pace on the Sunshine Coast will make you feel like you're on an island – even if, geographically speaking, that's not technically true. (It's really a coastal section of the mainland that's only accessible by boat.) Lean in to the laid-back vibe with a road trip around the region's remote communities. Our ideal itinerary? Gibsons for a brewery tour, Sechelt for a hike through Hidden Grove, and Robert's Creek for a spot of gallery-hopping.

East of Squamish, Watersprite Lake has been a favorite spot with locals ever since the BC Mountaineering Club built a hut here back in 2017. The lake's not for the unprepared: you definitely need a good 4WD vehicle to get to the trailhead, and from there it's a steep (but beautiful) hike up to the lake itself. But the reward is one of the region's most picturesque lakes. Even better: it's well off the tourist trail, so you'll feel like you have the place to yourself.

GOLDEN EARS PROVINCIAL PARK

1.5-hour drive from the city; https://bcparks.ca

There are so many reasons to love this vast provincial park. There's the excellent hiking, horseback riding, and swimming in Alouette Lake for starters. And then there's the incredible birdlife (look out for herons and golden eagles). But the main thing that keeps us coming back? The towering, moss-covered trees. An afternoon of forest bathing in their awe-inspiring presence is one of the most soothing balms around.

GULF ISLANDS

2.5-hour drive from the city, including ferry ride to Salt Spring Island; https://southerngulfislands.com

Peppered across the Salish Sea just off the mainland lie the 200 islands and islets that make up the Gulf Islands. Only 12 of these are inhabited, and each one of those 12 is a haven of tranquility. Think sleepy seaside towns full of creative artisans and bountiful organic farms bursting with produce. Picking which island to visit can be a tough call. Sea kayakers will tell you to go to Galiano and hikers

Try it!
GO SEA KAYAKING

Montague Harbour on Galiano Island is a fabulous spot to kayak from. Rent kayaks at the dock and ask for instructions to get to "seal" rock, where you're likely to spot dozens of sleek seals basking in the sun.

always rave about Mayne, but we say Salt Spring is usually a good place to start. It's got a handy direct ferry, plus lots of cute boutiques and delicious craft food and drink spots.

PEMBERTON

2.5-hour drive from the city; https://tourismpembertonbc.com

It may be just 15 miles (24 km) up the road from Whistler, but Pemberton feels another world away — and another era away, too. This idyllic farming village channels some seriously cozy small-town vibes, thanks to a smattering of mom-and-pop stores and little delis specializing in local produce. Of course, the village wouldn't be complete without a traditional diner. After a day hitting the local hiking, biking, and horseback riding trails, the burgers at Mile One Eating House are just the type of old-school comfort food you need.

» Don't leave without visiting The Beer Farmers, a craft brewery that grows its own barley and hops.

HELL'S GATE

1.5-hour drive from the city; www.hellsgateairtram.com

Don't let the name throw you — the vast gorge known as Hell's Gate is heavenly (and even the drive up to it is stunning). Here, the walls of the Fraser Canyon suddenly narrow, forcing the river into a frothing, thunderous rush of white water. Board the Airtram for a bird's eye view — and spare a thought for Simon Fraser, the 19th-century explorer who gave the gorge its name after a terrifying journey through it by canoe.

Solo, Pair, Crowd

Day to yourself? Bestie in town? Planning a getaway with the gang? Whoever you're with, there's plenty to explore outside Vancouver.

FLYING SOLO
Island solitude

Just a 20-minute ferry ride from Horseshoe Bay, scenic Bowen Island makes a great solo trip. Walk the steep path up to Artisan Square before rewarding your efforts with some goodies from the charming shops.

IN A PAIR
City break

Rain, coffee, seafood – Seattle is a home away from home for Vancouverites. Invite a pal on a 2.5-hour cross-border road trip for a Pacific Northwest weekend US-style.

FOR A CROWD
Splashing around

Gather your friends for an action-packed getaway at Harrison Lake. Race each other on a Sea-Doo, tackle the obstacle course at the giant inflatable water park, or kayak up the Harrison River.

VICTORIA

3-hour drive from the city, including ferry ride;
www.tourismvictoria.com

A getaway from Vancouver doesn't always mean venturing into the great outdoors. It's often just as tempting to hop on a ferry over to Victoria, out on Vancouver Island, with a truly relaxing weekend in mind. As the official Brunch Capital of Canada (according to Food Network, at least), Victoria is tailor-made for lazy mornings filled with glasses of mimosa and plates piled high with pancakes and French toast. There's also the pretty Butchart Gardens and the Royal BC Museum to explore – if you're still able to move after all that breakfast, of course.

» Don't leave without exploring Victoria's small but charismatic Chinatown; look out for Fan Tan Alley, Canada's narrowest street.

TOFINO

5.5-hour drive from the city, including ferry ride to Nanaimo;
www.tourismvictoria.com

In case the 5.5-hour travel time didn't give it away, Tofino definitely isn't a day trip. But it's a beloved surfing destination that's totally worth the journey. And besides, the trip there is part of the fun. You get to whale-watch on the ferry over to Nanaimo, then take a super-scenic drive to the western coast of Vancouver Island. Once you're there, the vibe couldn't be more relaxed. Days are spent catching waves from the endlessly long beaches, while evenings slip by in a magical haze of sunset watching and gorging on fish tacos. For that, we'd drive double the distance.

RICE LAKE ROAD

Lynn Creek

Lynn Canyon Park

Finish at the
END OF THE LINE
GENERAL STORE
Reward yourself with a
homemade treat, and check
out some local art and
souvenirs while you're there.

5

4

Take the plunge at the
30 FOOT POOL
Though freezing cold, the
emerald-green waters are
enticing enough to make
this a favorite swimming
hole in summer.

LYNN VALLEY ROAD

Lynn Canyon Park

Cross the iconic
LYNN CANYON SUSPENSION BRIDGE
At 160 ft (50 m), the bouncing bridge over the rushing
Lynn Creek canyon certainly isn't for the faint of heart.

2

1

Start at the
ECOLOGY CENTRE
Learn about the park's
fascinating history, watch an
educational puppet show with
the kids, or just grab a map.

PETERS   ROAD

LYNN
VALLEY

3

Hike to
TWIN FALLS
A short bridge will take
you over two stunning
turquoise waterfalls (this one
doesn't swing with every
step, we promise).

DUVAL ROAD

ROSS ROAD

0 meters   200
0 yards   200

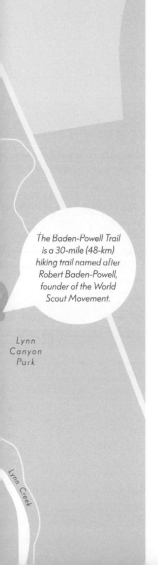

The Baden-Powell Trail is a 30-mile (48-km) hiking trail named after Robert Baden-Powell, founder of the World Scout Movement.

Lynn
Canyon
Park

Lynn Creek

A morning hike in
Lynn Canyon

Of course, no trip to Vancouver would be complete without a hike, and Lynn Canyon is one of the best places to get a taste of the North Shore's great outdoors. With steep canyon walls, turquoise rivers, and towering pines, it's a favorite among locals looking for a bit of fresh air. And getting here is a breeze; just hop on a bus from Granville Street and you'll be among the trees and trails in just over an hour. This tour covers the main Lynn Canyon highlights, but you can extend your walk into a full day trip if you're eager to keep exploring the area.

1. Ecology Centre
3663 Park Road;
www.ecologycentre.ca
///prevents.kingdom.volume

2. Lynn Canyon
Suspension Bridge
3363 Park Road
///marble.targeted.ally

3. Twin Falls
Between Baden-Powell Trail and Centennial Trail
///prickly.sailing.frocks

4. 30 Foot Pool
Baden-Powell Trail
///monopoly.contacts.doted

5. End of the Line
General Store
4193 Lynn Valley Road
///parting.that.fixture

With a little research and preparation, this city will feel like a home away from home. Check out these websites to ensure a healthy, safe stay in Vancouver.

Vancouver
DIRECTORY

SAFE SPACES

Vancouver is known for being a diverse and accepting city, though if you should ever feel uneasy or that you need to find your community, there are spaces and resources to help you out.

www.coastalchurch.org

A multicultural and interfaith society that offers outreach and community support at the Unitarian Church of Vancouver.

www.qmunity.ca

A nonprofit organization that focuses on outreach, initiatives, and services for queer, trans, and Two-Spirit folks.

www.womenshealthcollective.ca

A center offering programs, services, information, and activities to anyone who identifies as a woman, focusing on health and wellness support.

www.vlmfss.ca

This multicultural organization offers minorities support; staff are multilingual.

HEALTH

Canada has a universal healthcare system for its citizens, but if you're visiting from out of the country make sure you have a comprehensive health insurance policy.

www.providencehealthcare.org/hospitals-residences/st-paul%27s-hospital

Vancouver's central hospital offers emergency and medical services.

www.forvancouverlovers.com/en/best/24-hour-pharmacies-in-vancouver

A list of 24-hour and late-night pharmacies in Vancouver.

www.healthlinkbc.ca
Receive non-emergency health advice via a phoneline (811), website, or app.

www.checkhimout.ca
This nonprofit health initiative for gay, bi, and queer men offers counseling, testing, and other health-related services.

www.bcwomens.ca
A health organization offering services for women, newborns, and families.

TRAVEL SAFETY INFORMATION
Before and during your stay, check out this list of resources to help ensure you have a safe trip.

www.bccdc.ca/health-info/ diseases-conditions
Consult this website for a list of clinics that offer treatment for various illnesses.

www.vpd.ca/report-a-crime
Victim services and support provided by the Vancouver Police Department. Non-emergency crimes can be reported online.

www.emergencyinfobc.gov.bc.ca
The latest information in severe weather or local emergencies, evacuation details, and response and recovery resources.

ACCESSIBILITY
Vancouver is a world leader when it comes to accessibility, with most venues and services available to all. These resources will help to make your journey go smoothly.

www.hellobc.com/stories/ accessible-vancouver
Insider tips on visiting Vancouver's main sights and taking public transportation when mobility is a consideration.

www.vancouver.ca/people-programs/accessible-city.aspx
A list of accessibility information and initiatives from the City of Vancouver.

www.destinationvancouver.com/ plan-your-trip/accessible-vancouver
An accessible travel guide to Vancouver and the surrounding area for people with visual, hearing, and mobility impairments.

www.wheelchairtraveling.com/ vancouver-canada-accessible-attractions-activities-travel-wheelchair
A list of wheelchair-accessible sights in and around Vancouver, and tips for getting around the city for those with impaired mobility.

INDEX

ACKNOWLEDGMENTS

Meet the illustrator

Award-winning British illustrator David Doran is based in a studio by the sea in Falmouth, Cornwall. When not drawing and designing, David tries to make the most of the beautiful area in which he's based; sea-swimming all year round, running the coastal paths and generally spending as much time outside as possible.

Main Contributors Lindsay Anderson, Vivian Chung, Aleem Kassam, Jacqueline Salomé, Michael White

Senior Editor Lucy Richards

Senior Designer Vinita Venugopal

Project Editor Elspeth Beidas

US Editor Jennette ElNaggar

Editors Alex Pathe, Danielle Watt

Designer Jordan Lambley

Proofreader Kathryn Glendenning

Indexer Helen Peters

Senior Cartographic Editor Casper Morris

Cartography Manager Suresh Kumar

Cartographer Ashif

Jacket Designers Jordan Lambley, Sarah Snelling

Jacket Illustrator David Doran

Senior Production Editor Jason Little

Senior Production Controller Samantha Cross

Managing Editor Hollie Teague

Managing Art Editor Sarah Snelling

Art Director Maxine Pedliham

Publishing Director Georgina Dee

First edition 2023

Published in Great Britain by Dorling Kindersley Limited, DK, One Embassy Gardens, 8 Viaduct Gardens, London SW11 7BW, UK

The authorised representative in the EEA is Dorling Kindersley Verlag GmbH. Arnulfstr. 124, 80636 Munich, Germany

Published in the United States by DK Publishing, 1745 Broadway, 20th Floor, New York, NY 10019, USA

Copyright © 2023 Dorling Kindersley Limited
A Penguin Random House Company
23 24 25 26 10 9 8 7 6 5 4 3 2 1

The publishers cannot accept responsibility for any consequences arising from the use of this book, nor for any material on third party websites, and cannot guarantee that any website address in this book will be a suitable source of travel information.

A CIP catalog record for this book is available from the British Library.

A catalog record for this book is available from the Library of Congress.

ISSN: 1542 1554
ISBN: 9780 2416 3306 9

Printed and bound in China.

www.dk.com

MIX
Paper | Supporting responsible forestry
FSC™ C018179
www.fsc.org

This book was made with Forest Stewardship Council™ certified paper – one small step in DK's commitment to a sustainable future. **For more information go to www.dk.com/our-green-pledge**

A NOTE FROM DK EYEWITNESS

The world is fast-changing and it's keeping us folk at DK Eyewitness on our toes. We've worked hard to ensure that this edition of Vancouver Like a Local is up-to-date and reflects today's favorite places but we know that standards shift, venues close and new ones pop up in their place. So, if you notice something has closed, we've got something wrong, or left something out, we want to hear about it. Please drop us a line at travelguides@dk.com